Entering Zen

Other Books by Ben Howard

POETRY

Leaf, Sunlight, Asphalt
(Salmon Poetry, 2009)

Dark Pool
(Salmon Poetry, 2004)

Midcentury
(Salmon Poetry, 1997)

Lenten Anniversaries: Poems 1982–1989
(The Cummington Press, 1990)

Northern Interior: Poems 1975–1982
(The Cummington Press, 1986)

Father of Waters: Poems 1965–1976
(Abattoir Editions: University of Nebraska at Omaha, 1979)

PROSE

The Pressed Melodeon: Essays on Modern Irish Writing
(Story Line Press, 1996)

Entering Zen

Ben Howard

WHITLOCK PUBLISHING

ALFRED, NY

Entering Zen by Ben Howard

First Whitlock Publishing edition 2011

Whitlock Publishing
P.O. Box 472
Alfred, NY 14802

ISBN 10: 0-9770956-7-3
ISBN 13: 978-0-9770956-7-4

This book was set in Dante on 55# acid-free paper that meets ANSI standards for archival quality.

Printed in the United States of America.

In memory of
Carol Ruth Burdick
(1928 – 2008)

CONTENTS

Preface xi

Foreword xv

Let's Get Meditating 1

Ichigo Ichie 4

Village of Water 7

Zenlike Peace 10

Orangeburg 13

Habit Energies 16

Of Fountain Pens and Emptiness 19

Sitting without Goals 22

Just This 25

Zen and the Classifieds 28

Mindful Wading 31

At the Salvation Army.. 34

Cooking with Dogen 37

Springwater 40

Innocence 43

Firewood and Ashes 46

Stability and Resilience 49

The Cypress in the Garden 52

Mountains and Rivers 55

Snobbery... 58

Just Sitting 61

The Tow Rope 64

Being with Dying.. 67

108 Delusions 70

Ice Dams 73

Not-Knowing 76

Preferences 79

Attention, Attention, Attention! 82

As Surely as One's Shadow 85

The Mother Road 88

A Single Gentian 91

The Thoughtless People 94

A Sense of Ceremony 97

What is This? 100

Stepping Stones 103

Seven Words 106

Me and Mu 109

Without Ideals or Violence 112

Travels 115

Resting 118

The Way It Is 121

Taking Care 124

Awareness and Conjecture 127

A Mighty Wave 130

Closing Doors 133

Chazen Ichimi 136

The Tempo of Meditation 139

Weathered Wood 142

Silence and Intimacy 145

A Sense of Arrival 148

Dropping into Awareness 151

Looking Deeply 154

A Fundamental Perplexity 157

Dappled Things 160

Carols, Hymns, and Chants 163

CB's List 166

Leaving Things Alone 169

The Sword of Attention 172

To Study the Self 175

From Rouge to the Color of Moonlight 178

Batter Up 181

Saying Nothing 184

Here and There 188

Closing the Gap 191

Pursuing the Real 194

Back to School 198

The Sound of Tea 202

The Leaves' Fossils 205

What Were You Thinking? 209

Hope is Not a Plan 212

Children from the Sun 216

The Life I Have Been Given 220

Habits of Mind 224

Leaning into the Curves 228

Effortless Effort 232

Notes 237

About the Author 249

Preface

*L*ate in the ninth century, a monk named Kyosho asked the Zen master Gensha how to enter Zen.

"Can you hear the murmuring of the mountain stream?" asked Gensha.

"Yes," Kyosho replied.

"Then enter there."

With that response, we are told, Kyosho experienced a spontaneous awakening.

Here in the twenty-first century, there are innumerable ways of entering Zen. The sound of water is one, the flow of the breath another. But there is also the icon on your computer screen, the glowing map on your GPS, the verbal nugget arriving via Twitter. All afford opportunities to be present. All can conduce to awakening. And all are means by which to cultivate the clarity, stability of mind, and equanimity that are the first fruits of meditative practice. Over time, that practice can lead the dedicated practitioner out of the dream of a separate self and into the reality of present life, where everything is impermanent, and everything is connected. By so doing, the practice can also engender wisdom and compassion, the larger aims of Zen training.

The essays in this collection represent seventy-five ways of entering Zen. Written from the vantage point of a committed lay practitioner, the essays first appeared as biweekly columns in the *Alfred Sun*, the community newspaper of the village of Alfred, New York. They have since been posted on my blog, "One Time, One Meeting" (www.practiceofzen.wordpress.com). Although their initial purpose was educational, and their early forms were brief, they have evolved into a kind of *samu*, or work practice, in which I have attempted to present and clarify aspects of Zen practice for myself and others. Part almanac, part memoir, and part primer on meditation, this collection is addressed to anyone who might wish to take up the practice of meditation, or deepen an existing practice, or explore the nuances and complexities of Zen teachings.

For their insights as well as their collective example, I am indebted to the many teachers quoted in these pages. I should also like to thank all those who encouraged and supported this effort, including readers of the *Alfred Sun*, who sometimes made useful suggestions for future columns. Special thanks to Tim and Pat Bancroft, Barry Briggs, Frank Bunke, Galen Brooks, Sharon Burdick, Shinge Roko Sherry Chayat Roshi, Art Couchman, Tynette Deveaux, Allen Grove, Roshi Joan Halifax, Sharon Hoover, Joyce Howland, Siobhan Hutson, Jeanne Hyland, Jasmine Lellock, Alan and Caroline Littell, David Meissner, Andrea Miller, John L. Murphy, Gary Ostrower, Tom Peterson, Amanda Pustilnik,

David Snyder, Emrys Westacott, and Heather Yanda. And, not least, thanks to my son, Alexander Benjamin Howard, who prodded me to put these essays online, and to my wife, Robin Caster Howard, who listened patiently to draft after draft, week after week, as I endeavored to bring my sometimes inchoate thoughts into accord with things as they are.

—Ben Howard
Alfred, New York
March, 2011

Foreword

*H*ow can we convey the essence of an experience in words, without losing the vitality of that experience? So often language itself deadens what was intensely alive, or renders it unrecognizable, distorted by conceptualization. How can we communicate that which cannot be defined or confined in words? Thus the Zen saying, "It's like a mute person with a dream," or the Taoist dictum, "One who knows does not speak; one who speaks does not know." Third Zen Ancestor Sosan Ganchi, in his poem "On Believing in Mind," warned us, "Wordiness and intellection—the more with them, the further away we go."

When logical constructs fail, what then? We can turn to poetry, which can circumvent the handicaps of conceptualization through surprising turns of phrase and indirect currents of thought; and we can turn to the direct expressions, illogical yet charged with life-changing insights, found in Zen koans and teaching stories. Both require a willingness to immerse ourselves in the language of intimacy, the practice of awareness.

So when we discover the words of a poet who is also a long-time practitioner of Zen, we find ourselves in a rewarding realm indeed. The work of Ben Howard in this engaging book offers just such a realm. Using his own observations of nature and the nature of reality, interspersed with pithy quotations from contemporary and ancient Zen masters as well as lines from poets, baseball players, neighbors, and friends, Howard has written a refreshingly unpretentious, down-home account of the practice of Zen. He warns of the danger of naming things, yet offers a clear-eyed investigation into how language can, indeed, express the ineffable. He illuminates personal epiphanies in a way that brings us fully into the realm of pure experience, beyond duality.

Quoting Jane Hirshfield and her use of a line by the Japanese poet Myoe ("Bright, bright, bright, bright, the moon"), he exhorts us to see that dualism can be transcended, that "the self's isolation may be overcome." Just listen, he urges; then, let the words come out of that silence, and they will be eloquent words indeed. With his wry humor and quiet humility, he demonstrates that ordinary language can be fresh and refreshing.

Howard ponders the essential Zen experience—kensho, or seeing one's true nature—and cautions that one cannot make of it a goal. Rather, he notes, it is the pure attentiveness to the moment that allows the seasoned practitioner to break through all ideas of gain, of self-improvement, to the vastness of realization.

Taking a simple word like "rely," he plumbs definitions and allusions to discover a fundamental independence (what Zen refers to as "that One shining alone") within a world of interdependence. As the *Diamond Sutra* reminds us, we must "rely upon that mind which alights upon nothing whatsoever." In so doing, we return, he says, "to absolute reality, the ground of being, from which all conditioned phenomena… are constantly arising."

Examining the world of interdependence, Howard notes how enmeshed we are in what Martin Luther King, Jr. called an "inescapable network of mutuality, tied into a single garment of destiny," and adds, "To deny that reality is to live in a self-centered dream—and to widen the gap between self and other." To close that perceived duality, we must bring a compassionate heart to that most universal of experiences—suffering, about which the Buddha taught in his first sermon after his awakening.

How to do that? Howard offers this: "For the Zen practitioner, the best medicine is meditation, which not only steadies the mind but also affords access to our internal suffering and its causes. To attend to others' suffering, Zen teachings tell us, we must first attend to our own. This directive is not a prescription for self-pity or an invitation to wallow in our woes. Rather, it is an admonition to become aware of the elements in our psyches and our culture that engender suffering—the craving, fear, and anger; the impulse to violence; the mindless consumption; the habitual patterns of reactivity."

How difficult it is to attend to our own suffering—to be with it as it is, without turning away! Automatically, we seek to be elsewhere, anywhere but here. Indeed, inattentiveness and a concomitant craving for distraction are among the most habitual of patterns. In fact, we rarely notice how removed we are from the present moment. To prove this point, Howard offers an exercise to the reader: "I suggest that you sit still for three minutes and count the number of thoughts you have during that time. Then sit still for another three minutes, labeling your thoughts ('Thinking about tomorrow's meeting'; 'thinking about last night'). You may well find that the bulk of your thoughts pertain not to the present but to the past or the future: to where you have been or where you might sometime be."

To enter into this present moment, we need no special devices, no memorized affirmations, no exotic mantras. We simply have to let go of everything extraneous—what we think regarding this moment, what we add to it, or try to take away from it. This practice of being here for our lives requires nothing but a disciplined willingness to return home to the present again and again until it becomes our natural way of being. As Howard so clearly conveys in *Entering Zen*, all we need is already right here.

—Shinge Roko Sherry Chayat Roshi, Abbot,
Dai Bosatsu Zendo and the Zen Center of Syracuse

Let's Get Meditating

*T*welve years ago, some friends and I formed a sitting group in the community of Alfred, New York. Our intent was to provide a place of stillness and silence and to cultivate the practices of sitting and walking meditation, as taught by the Vietnamese Zen master Thich Nhat Hanh. Some of us brought prior experience in Eastern meditation. All of us brought our Western conditioning.

So it was with one of our number, an anxious former New Yorker, who arrived one Sunday evening looking unusually impatient.

"Well," said he, rubbing his hands and bouncing from one foot to the other, "let's get meditating."

As we later learned, Barbara Walters was interviewing Monica Lewinsky at nine o'clock that evening, and he didn't want to miss a word.

In his general outlook if not his specific motive, our friend was not alone. On the contrary, American culture has been described as always *en route* to somewhere else, always busy and always in a hurry. And with the advent of e-mail, Twitter, and other forms of advanced technology, our habitual rush into the future has grown more furious than ever. Meditation is supposed to be about "stopping and looking"—or at least about slowing down. But to those attached to ceaseless forward movement, even an hour devoted to stopping and looking can become one more step on the way to somewhere else.

The desire to be in some other place, and to get there as soon as possible, is both a symptom and a cause of a general anxiety, driving us into the future even as we fear it. Over the past decade a wide variety of people, including students, faculty, social workers, police, and clergy, have attended our Sunday-evening sessions. Some have come out of boredom, curiosity, loneliness, or a desire to find a deeper meaning in their lives. But the root motive is often anxiety, which Thich Nhat Hanh has called the endemic illness of Western culture. *Better get moving*, its voices tell us. *Better get meditating*.

Zen meditation is not a panacea for anxiety, as sometimes thought, nor is it a drug-free cure. But the practice can provide an antidote, a countervailing force in our busy-busy lives. In the simplest form of Zen meditation, we sit as still and upright as we can manage, doing nothing but following the flow of our breath and paying attention to whatever is occurring, within us and around us. We note the tensions in our bodies, the eruption of a voice down the hall. We note a passing thought—*where are my car keys?*—or a remembered image. And we observe those impulses that urge us to keep moving—to *get meditating*—and hurl us into the future. When we have sat for awhile, our bodies begin to settle, and our thoughts arrive at a slower pace. And as we stop trying to control our environment, our immediate surroundings present themselves with greater clarity and vivacity. We feel more alive as well as more relaxed.

Such are the immediate benefits of Zen meditation, which may be felt in a matter of weeks. But it would be a mistake to think of Zen practice as merely a stress-reduction technique, or a mode of self-improvement, or a way of escaping from the world. The reduction of stress might better be viewed as a point of entry—a portal into an ancient contemplative practice. Over time, that practice teaches us to appreciate our lives, however hurried or fragmented their present state, and to align our anxious minds with things as they are, not as we would have them be. And rather than isolate us, the practice deepens our connection with other people.

I intend to say more about these matters in future essays. In the meantime, let's get meditating.

January 31, 2008

Ichigo Ichie

*F*or the Westerner who might wish to enter Zen practice, one of the most accessible points of entry is the way of words. Over the centuries Zen teachers have warned against reliance on language, likening it to a finger pointing to the moon, but they have also offered pithy sayings, ranging from the most intelligible to the most arcane. "Not always so," Suzuki Roshi observed. "Only don't know," the Korean master Seung Sahn declared. "Live as if you were dead," exhorted the seventeenth-century Rinzai master Shido Bunan. Taken to heart, any one of these sayings might initiate the newcomer into the practice of Zen. For my own part, however, I have found the Japanese motto *ichigo ichie* to be one of the most helpful, both for the novice and the seasoned practitioner.

Pronounced *each-ee-go each-ee-ay* and translated as "one time, one meeting," this motto is closely associated with the Japanese tea ceremony. *Ichigo ichie* enjoins the host and guests in the tea hut to regard their gathering as unprecedented and

4

unrepeatable. Though governed by custom and tradition, each meeting is unique. It will not occur again.

Ichigo ichie is said to have originated with Ii Naosuke, tea master and chief administrator of the Tokugawa Shogunate. Every morning, Naosuke, who had many enemies and feared assassination, made himself a bowl of tea, pronouncing it *ichigo ichie*: unprecedented and unrepeatable. In 1860 Naosuke was indeed assassinated, but the phrase he coined survived him, becoming a motto for students of the Way of Tea.

"One time, one meeting" is also a motto for students of Zen meditation, but in Zen practice the context extends well beyond the drinking of tea. For in Zen training we learn to regard *all* encounters as unprecedented and unrepeatable, however similar they appear. In her essay "There Are No Repetitions," the Rinzai priest and concert pianist Maurine Stuart puts the matter this way:

> We are always at the beginning. It is always the very first time. When I play the piano I often come to a repeat sign. Can that passage be repeated? If I am teaching a piano student and we see a repeat sign, I tell the student that there are no repeats. We return to the beginning of a certain passage, but it's never the same. It's always fresh.

At first glance, these assertions may seem to defy common sense. Would that the menus of certain restaurants might be unrepeatable! Would that our waiter, putting our food on the table, might say something other than "there you go." Would that Garrison Keillor's tone of voice might vary even a little, or the village siren play a new tune. *Same old, same old,* we complain. *Been there, done that.*

5

To the Zen practitioner, however, such dismissals only mask an underlying reality. The menu may not change, but other conditions will, and no two meals will ever be the same. By marshaling such phrases as "same old, same old," we strengthen our preconceptions and bolster our sense of security, but we also erect a verbal screen between ourselves and the world before us.

To pierce that screen is the task of the Zen practitioner. And to return to the ground of being, where we may experience the world afresh, is a central aim of Zen discipline. Sitting still without thought of attainment, we relinquish our preconceptions and renew our attention to whatever is occurring, right here, right now: the flow of our breath, the rumble of a truck, the thought of an errand left undone. In so doing, we free ourselves from our habitual patterns of thought and feeling, our sometimes painful attachments to the past. And we allow the things of this world to reveal themselves as they truly are: vibrant, unprecedented, and unrepeatable.

February 14, 2008

Village of Water

About ten years ago, I wrote a check for $57.00 to the Village of Water. At the time, I was attempting to pay my water bill. Oblivious of my oversight, I mailed the check, and somehow the Village of Alfred managed to cash it. When the bank returned the canceled check, as banks used to do, I discovered my blunder.

What was I thinking? I asked myself. Or as my mother would have said, *Whatever possessed you?* The script was neat, the handwriting definitely mine. The check bore my signature. But whoever wrote the "Village of Water" was miles away at the time.

However extreme, my error was not uncommon. Nor was it peculiar to professors. Quite possibly, the chickadees at our feeder and the deer who eat our dogwoods live continuously in the present. They have to. But we human beings have the option of being elsewhere, and that elsewhere is often the future or the past. And when we are not revisiting the past or rehearsing the future, we are often absorbed in abstract thought.

To return us to the present moment is the first purpose of Zen meditation. The Vietnamese Zen master Thich Nhat Hanh describes the practice in this way:

> *Meditation means you have to be present in the present moment. If the body is here but the mind is wandering elsewhere, in that moment you're not present—you're not present for yourself, and you're not present for your husband, your children, your brothers or sisters, your nation, or your people. That is the opposite of meditation. Being present in the present moment means you are not being imprisoned by the past or sucked up by the future.*

As Thich Nhat Hanh further explains, being present in the present moment does not preclude reflection, planning, or visionary thought. Rather, it returns the wandering mind, which doesn't know it is wandering, to an awareness of whatever it is up to.

In Zen teachings, this capacity for being present is known as mindfulness, and it is an essential component of Zen discipline. Mindfulness may be cultivated in many ways, but at the beginning we can best develop it by sitting still, with our spines straight and the rest of our bodies relaxed. Maintaining that posture for ten, twenty, or thirty minutes, we bring a gentle, non-judgmental attention to our breath, our feelings, our passing thoughts, our changing states of mind. We become present for ourselves.

But can we also become present for other people? Beneficial though it is, the mindfulness cultivated in seated meditation is of limited value if it does not extend into our daily lives, where our presence—and often, our absence—profoundly affects others around us. "When you walk," Zen teachers tell us, "just walk." That admonishment directs us to give undivided attention to the one thing we are doing, be it cooking dinner, or writing a check, or listening to a friend. Mindfulness of this kind grows naturally from the habit of daily sitting, but it it may also be practiced by anyone at any time.

By way of demonstration, may I suggest that if you are drinking a cup of coffee while you are reading this column, put down your coffee and give full attention to the column. Or better yet, put down the column and give full attention to your coffee. Hold the cup in both hands, as Zen monks do, and inhale the aroma. Contemplate the origins, the history, and the nature of the drink you are about to ingest. Then drink your coffee, giving full attention to its taste. Continue this practice for a week or more, and see what you discover.

February 28, 2008

Zenlike Peace

*N*ot so long ago, the journalist Michael Crowley, who was covering Hillary Clinton's campaign for the *New Republic*, reported a conversation with the "makeup artist" in charge of preparing the candidates for the debates. Was Hillary a basket case, he asked, in those final moments before she went on? On the contrary, the makeup artist replied. "Sitting in the makeup chair seems to be one of the few moments of zenlike peace the candidates ever get."

Of all the images projected by the current presidential race, the spectacle of Hillary Clinton, John McCain, and the others sitting in "zenlike peace" in their makeup chairs is one of the more diverting. Yet if that image highlights a certain absurdity in the present campaign, it also reflects a popular view of Zen meditation. According to this view, to sit in *zazen* is to abide in perfect peace, untroubled by such things as one's perilous standing in the polls. In the serene mind of the Zen practitioner, such worrisome thoughts—and thoughts in general—

have ceased to exist, leaving a space as blank as an unmarked ballot.

Prevalent though they are, such perceptions of Zen attainment have little to do with the daily practice of Zen meditation. To be sure, Zen masters through the centuries have described the state of *satori*, in which ordinary, dualistic consciousness dissolves, and self and world become one. But as the modern Zen master Kosho Uchiyama warns us in his book *Opening the Hand of Thought*, "to think that people become great by doing zazen, or to think that you are going to *gain* satori, is to be sadly misled by your own illusion." For the aim of Zen practice is not to attain a state of continuous bliss or permanent contentment. Rather, it is to cultivate a clear and open awareness, within which transitory mental states, however calm or vexed, are recognized for what they are.

When practicing zazen, we adopt a stable, upright posture, aligning ourselves with the earth's gravitational force. We settle into stillness, and we rest in awareness. Within that sky-like awareness, thoughts arrive and depart, as if they were passing clouds. Some are luminous and wispy, others dense and dark. But if we remain in awareness and do not pursue them, our thought-clouds leave as readily as they came. Uchiyama calls this process "opening the hand of thought," and he describes it in this way:

> When we let go of our conceptions, there is no other possible reality than what is right now ... Dwelling here and now in this reality, letting go of all the accidental things that arise in our minds, is what I mean by "opening the hand of thought."

11

Uchiyama contrasts this state of open awareness with our usual state of mind, in which we grasp at the objects of our thoughts, fashioning scenarios to suit our needs.

The difference may be illustrated by a simple example. Let us imagine that as Hillary Clinton sat in her makeup chair before the New Hampshire debate she had the thought, "Don't forget to mention that Obama represented that louse Rezko in Chicago." Were she to have pursued that thought, rehearsing her remarks, anticipating Obama's response and planning her next move, she would merely have been thinking, strategically and analytically. She would have been living in the future. However, had she acknowledged her initial thought and let it go, returning to her breath and abiding in awareness, she would have indeed been cultivating a "zenlike peace," and she would have also been practicing Zen meditation.

March 13, 2008

Orangeburg

*I*f you are a homeowner in Alfred, New York, you may have heard of Orangeburg pipe. Widely used for drainage and sewer lines, it is best described as ten layers of tarpaper rolled up to form a pipe. Orangeburg takes its name from Orangeburg, New York, its point of manufacture. Properly seated in a bed of sand, Orangeburg might last fifty years. Or it might not.

Last month, I learned these facts the hard way. With little warning, our sewer line backed up, and our basement flooded. We called a plumber, and when his power snake brought back dirt, we knew we were in for some serious digging. Twenty-four hours later, in a trench where our lawn had been, we laid eyes on the cause of our misery. Sure enough, it was a length of Orangeburg pipe, flattened and degraded. Calling it a name not fit to print, I wondered why anyone would choose such a product, let alone trust it to last.

The answers weren't far to seek. Orangeburg pipe gained popularity in the decade after World War II, when iron and steel were in short supply. Contractors liked it because it was user-friendly and readily available. Homeowners liked it because it was cheap. By the standards of its day, it was a serviceable product, if hardly top of the line. That it would one day fall apart was the future homeowner's problem.

Whatever its merits as a plumbing component, Orangeburg pipe well illustrates a central focus of Zen training. For in Zen teachings we learn of "the impermanence of all conditioned things," whether those things be our sewer lines, our bodies, our thoughts, our relationships, or our very lives. And in Zen practice, we come to know the truth of impermanence through direct experience.

That all things change is hardly breaking news. A few years ago, as I was waiting for a TV show to resume, the words "Embrace change" flashed on the screen. While that sounded like something a Zen master might say, the purveyor of this advice turned out to be Rochester Gas and Electric. It would seem that awareness of impermanence has at long last entered the American mainstream.

Yet it is one thing to have a conceptual understanding of impermanence and quite another to experience it concretely. In Zen meditation we cultivate a continuous awareness of impermanence not through the contemplation of lofty verities but through an intimate contact with changes as they are unfolding, moment by moment and breath by breath. We notice that no two breaths are quite the same. And if we are really paying attention, we notice that everything is changing, including our sensations, thoughts, feelings, and states of mind. Neither we nor the world's bright things are as solid as we'd supposed.

It is not always pleasant to live with such awareness. We have every reason to resist it. Yet in the long run, if we can come to embody the truth of impermanence, we can align ourselves with the reality of change, and we can learn to live in harmony with its laws. For as Zen Master Thich Nhat Hanh reminds us, we suffer not because things are impermanent but because we expect them to be permanent when they are not. If we doubt that proposition, we have only to sit still for a while, following our breath and watching the changes within and around us.

Or, if we prefer, we can contemplate Orangeburg pipe.

March 27, 2008

Habit Energies

*P*icture, if you will, a horse and rider. The horse is galloping down a road, and the rider is hanging on for dear life.

"Where are you going?" calls a man from the side of the road.

"I don't know," answers the rider. "Ask the horse."

According to Zen teachings, the horse in this story represents the force of habit, or what Zen master Thich Nhat Hanh calls "habit energies." Whether we're aware of them or not, those energies drive our lives, even when we're sleeping. They rush us into the future, and we may feel powerless to stop them. In his poem "Habits" the American poet W.S. Merwin acknowledges as much. "Even in the middle of the night," he writes of his habits, "They go on handing me around."

I suspect that most of us are familiar with that experience. In my own case, I recall a Saturday afternoon when I found myself heading toward Wegman's, though I was supposed to be driving to the Valu Home Center to buy some paint. My horse was a Honda Accord, but the pattern was much the same.

Habits may be pleasant, healthful, and productive. They may also protect us, or comfort us during a crisis. But habits of mind can dull our sensibilities and distort our perceptions of other people. And in the arts, they can harden into stylistic tics and conceptual clichés, impeding the creative spirit. Perhaps that is why Nadia Boulanger, the legendary teacher and composer, once declared that she loved tradition but despised habit.

In Zen practice we do not despise habit or consign it to a mental perdition. We do not try to transcend it. Rather, we sit still, cultivating an awareness of our breath, our bodies, our changing mental states. Over time, we may notice that certain patterns of thought and feeling arise again and again. We acknowledge their presence, as we might acknowledge bits of songs that come and go."Hello, habit energies," says Thich Nhat Hanh to his own.

This is a simple but potent practice, and as it deepens, we may find that the force of our habits diminishes proportionately. Where before there was only the habit, now there is both the habit and our awareness. And as we become ever more mindful, we empower ourselves to form new and more wholesome habits—and to drop those that do us harm.

If we continue to cultivate such awareness, we may discover that our habits have roots deeper and broader than the personal. They are grounded in our histories, familial and social, and they are fed by contemporary culture. In totalitarian countries, people live with the habit of suspicion. In our own, we are living with the habit of fear, whether its object be sickness, aging, a destitute retirement, or a terrorist attack. Every night, the news and the Big Pharma ads nourish that habit of feeling.

Zen is no remedy for cultural illness. Nor is meditation a magic cure for long-term addictions. But if we are diligent, Zen practice can release us from ingrained, corrosive habits of mind. We don't have to drive to Wegman's every Saturday afternoon. We don't have to be afraid.

April 10, 2008

Of Fountain Pens and Emptiness

*T*oday I am writing this column with my Sailor 1911 fountain pen. Its name commemorates the origin of the Sailor Pen Company, which was founded in 1911 by Mr. Kyugoro Sakata of Hiroshima, Japan. Having learned about fountain pens from a British sailor, Mr. Sakata started his own company, naming it after his source of inspiration. My Sailor 1911 is plum-colored and sports a gold-plated nib, from which the black ink flows freely. A gift from my wife, it is a pleasure to use and a handsome object in its own right.

Yet my pen is also a composite thing, and when I take it apart to clean it, I see that it consists of four principal components: nib, cartridge, cap, and barrel. Were I to take those components themselves apart, I would discover that my fountain pen, which feels so stable in my hand, is actually an impermanent aggregate, to which the concept "fountain pen" has been applied. And though it appears independent, it is really a locus of interdependent causes and conditions, including the manufacturers who produced its resin, metal, and ink, the craftsman who assembled it, and of course Mr. Sakata himself. Far from being a separate entity, my pen might better be seen as an event in the ever-changing web of life. For all its beauty and functionality, it is void of solidity or intrinsic existence.

That is no small discovery. And were I to continue my investigation, examining my Sailor 1911 under an electron microsope, I would see that my so-called fountain pen is mostly energy and formless space. I would recognize the formlessness—or what Zen teachings call "emptiness"—beneath the form. Through direct experience, I would have verified the core teaching of the *Heart Sutra*, which is chanted daily in Zen monasteries. "Form is no other than emptiness," that sutra informs us, "emptiness no other than form." A pen is indeed a pen, but it is also not a pen. And what is true of fountain pens is true of all phenomena, ourselves included.

To examine the world and the self in this fashion might seem a rather negative, if not destructive, enterprise, but in practice it is quite the opposite. It is as nurturing as it is liberating. In his book *A New Earth*, Eckhart Tolle explains:

> *Once you realize and accept that all structures (forms) are unstable, even the seemingly solid material ones, peace arises within you. This is because the recognition of the impermanence of all forms awakens you to the dimension of the formless within yourself, that which is beyond death.*

In Zen teachings, what Tolle describes as the "dimension of the formless" is usually called the "absolute" dimension. It is contrasted with the "relative" dimension, where a pen is a pen and a post is a post. In Zen training we are enjoined to see all things, including our bodies, thoughts, and feelings, from both perspectives. We cultivate a kind of double vision, seeing the changing and the changeless, the relative and the absolute, as two sides of a single coin. By so doing, we loosen our anxious attachments to things and thoughts and feelings, having recognized that ultimately there is nothing solid to be attached to, or any need to be attached. And if peace arises, as it often does, it is because at long last we are seeing things as they are.

April 24, 2008

Sitting without Goals

*I*mre, a three-year-old friend of mine, delights in kicking things. When my wife and I gave him a set of educational blocks, of the sort that are supposed to develop eye-hand coordination, Imre took a few minutes to build a tower, then merrily kicked it across the room. Perhaps he was learning eye-foot coordination. Perhaps he has a future in the NFL.

One morning, Imre's mother invited us over for a Sunday brunch. As we and a few other grown-ups were tucking into a delicious custard pie, Imre decided it was time to run around the table, dragging his wooden train and yelling at the top of his lungs. It was difficult to hear ourselves think, let alone carry on a conversation.

Fortunately, I'd come prepared. Earlier that morning, as I was pouring my Cheerios into a bowl, a blue matchbox car dropped out of the box. Foreseeing its possible use, I had stashed it in my pocket.

Armed with that equipment, I stopped Imre in his tracks. "I have a present for you," I said, "but if you want it you will have to sit still for one minute."

Regarding me quizzically, Imre agreed to the deal, and for the next forty seconds, he sat more or less still, chuckling all the while. Apparently, sitting still struck him as a silly idea, but he was willing to go along. And having kept his end of the bargain, he received his car, which, he soon discovered, he could happily crash into the walls and furniture.

I tell this story partly to illustrate that sitting still, however rare it may be in our culture, is something even a rambunctious three-year-old can do. If you are reading this column, you must be older than three, and you can do it too.

However, if you are thinking that by doing Zen meditation you will receive an immediate reward, you may well be disappointed. It is true that even twenty minutes of *zazen* can leave us cleansed and refreshed. And over time, Zen practitioners experience such benefits as heightened clarity and concentration, sharpened intuition, and greater emotional stability. But to sit in zazen with goals and expectations is not only to invite frustration. It is also a sure-fire way to undermine one's effort.

In practicing Zen meditation, we sit still and return to the ground of being. We step back from our usual mental activities: defining, preferring, judging, or comparing this to that. Those activities may continue, but we merely watch them, and if we can, we drop them altogether. In so doing, we open ourselves to the experience of pure seeing, pure hearing, prior to names, goals, plans, and expectations. In the words of Zen master Kosho Uchiyama, we experience "what is there before [we] cook it up with thought." We enter the stream of life just as it is, not as we would have it be.

That is not so easily done. A lifetime of Western conditioning militates against it. But for those who persist, the practice of zazen becomes its own reward. In the language of Zen, by forgetting the self and its endless expectations, we "awaken to the ten thousand things." And whether those things be toy cars or custard pies, we see, hear, and taste them as never before.

May 8, 2008

Just This

*I*n the sometimes cryptic utterances of the Zen masters two plain words are often to be heard. Considered singly, they define two distinct aspects of Zen meditation. Considered together, they point to the core of the practice.

The first of these words is *just*, as in the Zen saying, "When you walk, just walk. When you eat, just eat."

In its most common adverbial usage, *just* means "no more than," and it serves to limit its object. "That's just George being George," we might say of an eccentric uncle. "Oh, that's just my arthritis acting up again," we might say to ourselves.

As used in Zen practice, *just* conveys a similar meaning, but it also connotes a wholehearted, one-pointed concentration. When you walk, just walk, giving full attention to your walking. When you eat, do the same. In contrast to so-called multi-tasking, the word *just* exhorts us to do one thing at a time, and to give undivided attention to whatever we are doing. A person washing the dishes *just to wash the dishes* is cultivating this quality of attention. A person watching CNN while walking on the treadmill is doing the very opposite.

No less than *just*, the pronoun *this* holds a promiment place in the lexicon of Zen. "*This* is everywhere," we read in the *Diamond Sutra*, "without differentiation or degree." "Zen is this," writes Roshi Bernie Glassman, "this moment, this stick, this thisness." The word may also be found in the Zen slogan "This is it" and the Zen koan "What is this?" In all of these instances, *this* adverts to whatever is present, right here, right now. More specifically, it refers to undifferentiated reality, prior to the imposition of concepts, opinions, or dualistic thinking generally.

Stepping outdoors in early March, we feel the heat of the sun. We may go on to check the thermometer, or describe the day as unseasonably warm, or attribute the unseasonable weather to global warming. But before any of that occurs, we feel the heat of the sun. By saying "this is it," we remind ourselves to be present for that transitory experience. And by asking "what is *this*?" (followed, in Zen training, with "I don't know"), we challenge our preconceptions and open ourselves to the depth of our experience.

Taken separately, *just* and *this* represent the two main components of meditative practice, which are often described as "stopping" (*samatha*) and "looking" (*vipassana*). Taken together, they form the slogan "just this," which, as James Austin observes in his *Zen-Brain Reflections,* offers a key to understanding and a practical tool for meditation. Practicing with *just*, we gather our energies; practicing with *this,* we bring our gathered energies to the penetration of reality. If the first trains us to focus on the one thing we are doing, the second invites us to look deeply into the present moment.

If you would like to try this practice, seat yourself in a comfortable, upright posture. Place your mind on your breathing. With your in-breath, say *just* silently to yourself. With your out-breath, say *this*. As you breathe in, feel the concentration of your energies; as you breathe out, surrender yourself to whatever you're experiencing. Continue this practice for several minutes, encountering *this, this, this,* just as it is.

May 22, 2008

Zen and the Classifieds

*I*f you have been reading this column, perhaps you have noticed that it sometimes appears across from the Classified Ads. Perhaps this has given you pause.

Zen is a meditative tradition of high purpose and great antiquity. What is a column on Zen doing across from an ad for Happy Jack Skin Balm? (Happy Jack "promotes healing and hair growth on dogs & cats without steroids!").

Zen is a late flowering of an even older spiritual tradition, whose foundational principles are known as the Four Noble Truths and the Noble Eightfold Path. What is a column on Zen doing across from an ad for Brown's Septic Service? ("Septic tanks pumped. Repairs and installations... Visa and MasterCard accepted").

Zen is concerned with the interdependence of all living beings, the impermanence of all conditioned things, and the suffering caused by a fundamental ignorance of reality. It is especially concerned with the Great Matter of life and death. What is a column on Zen doing across from ads for a floral-pattern love seat priced at $350, "I Love Alfred" bumper stickers at $1.50 each, and power scooters at "ABSOLUTELY NO COST TO YOU!!"?"

Nothing, one might say. If this column ends up across from the classifieds, it's because the editor of this paper, who was kind enough to include the column in the first place, had to put it somewhere.

A more accurate answer, however, is that Zen has everything to do with the classifieds—or, more broadly, with the mundane business of daily life. For unless one chooses to renounce our materialistic culture and become a monk or nun, Zen practice must somehow be integrated with a world where cats and dogs develop allergies, septic tanks need to be pumped, and love seats are bought and sold.

To be sure, meditative training is traditionally conducted in tranquil surroundings, where the lights are dim and the distractions few. Sitting quietly in the zendo, or perhaps at home in a space reserved for meditation, we settle into stillness. We learn to rest in simple presence, or what Zen calls the clear open sky of awareness. Thoughts cross our minds, but if we do not pursue them, they pass like clouds in the clear open sky. And when our sitting ends, we return to our lives feeling cleansed and refreshed.

Such respites nourish us, and they are not to be discounted. But the deeper value—and the higher challenge—of meditative practice lies in the integration of our experience in meditation with our experience of everyday life. With practice and proper training, we can learn to quiet our minds. We can learn to be still. But with patience and persistence, we can also learn to maintain stillness in the midst of external hubbub and meditative awareness in the midst of emotional turmoil.

In his new book, *The Wise Heart,* Jack Kornfield reminds us that there are "two distinct dimensions to our life: the ever-changing flow of experiences, and that which knows the experiences." Cultivating the latter, we can learn to trust in "that which knows": in an awareness that isn't angry when we are angry or depressed when we're depressed. It is merely present, sustaining us through joy and sorrow alike. Within that spacious awareness, pleasant and not-so-pleasant mind states come and go, as do the cats and dogs, the love seats and power scooters of our quotidian world. Aware of them all, we enlarge our sense of self. Embracing them all, we renew our connection with life.

June 5, 2008

Mindful Wading

I have a friend who's obssessed with fish. Or, more precisely, he's obsessed with fly fishing. So far as I can tell, when he is not fishing, he is thinking about fish. His license plate reads "Red Trout." So does his e-mail alias. I suspect that he also dreams about fish, and when he closes his eyes it's not Renoir's bathers or Rubens' nudes but red trout that swim up to greet him.

As some of you may have guessed, I am speaking of Richard Thompson, a painter of national renown, who recently retired from the School of Art and Design at Alfred University. Now he devotes his days to painting and fishing in (I think) that order.

Not long ago, Richard painted a series of pictures entitled "Mindful Wading." These paintings feature a fly fisherman in hat and waders making his way across a stream. The paintings were inspired by a conversation with my wife (who suggested to Richard that he take up yoga and meditation) and informed by Zen master Thich Nhat Hanh's *The Long Road Turns to Joy,* a pocket guide to walking meditation. As Thich

31

Nhat Hanh explains, "Walking meditation is walking just for the sake of walking." Mindful wading is Richard's version of the practice.

In one of Richard's paintings, a circular panel called "Cross Currents," the fisherman stands in the center with outstretched arms. In one hand he holds his rod, in the other his line. His feet are poised on the bed of the stream, surrounded by rocks, and he appears to be stepping gingerly, lest he stumble and fall. Above his head and to either side, the heads of trout are surfacing, each lunging toward a fly. Superimposed on five contrasting colors—yellow, red, blue, and two shades of green—the image feels both centered and kinetic. Viewed from a distance, the painting itself resembles a pinwheel.

"I fly fish," Richard has written, "and I wade streams. When I am crossing a stream I can't see the bottom, and the water is moving. I have to balance myself while testing each rock for stability. I do this navigating under low light and in bad weather and often on unfamiliar streams. I do mindful wading."

Thich Nhat Hanh might be surprised to learn of Richard's adaptation of his practice, but I suspect that he would approve. For the practice of walking meditation, as interpreted by Thich Nhat Hanh, is more than a respite from the rigors of zazen. It is a practice in its own right, whose purpose is to cultivate awareness of our bodies, our surroundings, and our changing states of mind. Beyond that, it is also a way of developing inner peace and a non-violent attitude toward our natural environment. Walking mindfully, we notice whether our steps are anxious or peaceful, and we cultivate the latter.

If you would like to practice walking meditation, select a place where you will not be observed or disturbed. Open your senses to your surroundings. Assume an upright but flexible posture, letting your shoulders drop and your belly soften. Relax into your breathing. Then walk naturally and unhurriedly, as though you had no destination, feeling the bottoms of your feet pressing the ground. Continue this practice for fifteen minutes or more, maintaining mindfulness all the while. If your mind wanders, gently bring it back.

As you become more skillful in this practice, you may wish to extend it into the public arena, increasing the tempo so as not to call attention to yourself. Let the practice restore your peace, your grace, and your dignity, as you walk—or wade—through your day.

June 19, 2008

At the Salvation Army

*I*f you have spent much time in a Salvation Army store, you may have heard a peculiar sound.

I heard it one afternoon when I accompanied my wife, Robin, to the Salvation Army Depot in Hornell. As Robin eagerly examined the dresses and blouses, hoping to find something from J. Jill or Eileen Fisher, I cast a desultory look at the polo shirts and tee-shirts, the vests and forlorn tweeds. Finding little to whet my appetite, I turned my attention to the sounds in the store.

What I heard was a low, continuous scraping. Was it a knife being sharpened? A blade removing paint? The sound was metallic, arhythmic, and vaguely abrasive, but it held my attention, in a way that the polo shirts had not. What was I hearing? Was it someone pushing a rusty cart down the aisle?

A few moments later, the answer dawned on me. What I was hearing was the sound of metal hangers—as many as a dozen—being pushed along metal rods, as the shoppers looked for bargains. From time to time the sound would diminish, as someone found a promising item. Then it would pick up again. The more I listened, the more varied and pleasing the sound became. Although it had probably always been there, I had never noticed it before.

Quite possibly I was listening because I had nothing better to do. But to listen to what is occurring, within and without, is an important aspect of Zen training. And to listen without immediately knowing—or trying to know—what one is hearing is itself an instructive practice.

It is natural, of course, to want to name what we hear. Unidentified sounds, particularly loud or sudden sounds, can be disconcerting, as Alfred Hitchcock well understood. When something goes bump in the night, it unnerves us, at least until we discern that it was not an intruder but the snow shovel falling and hitting the deck. Having solved that mystery, we can go back to sleep.

In Zen practice, however, the point is to be awake: to be aware of whatever is going on, moment by moment, and to be intimate with our experience. Our accumulated knowledge, however valuable, can stand in the way of that objective, as can our habits of defining, naming, and comparing. To have a concept of a sound is one thing, to have an experience of that sound another. The concept may give us comfort, but the experience returns us to the reality of our lives.

Waking at six in the morning, we hear the song of a bird. Is it a house wren? A Carolina wren? Some kind of warbler?

Listening again, we drop the effort to know what we are hearing—or to show off our knowledge to ourselves. We enjoy a moment of wonder and pure listening. In the language of Zen, we savor the "suchness" of the song, its transitory presence in the stream of time.

Such moments are central to Zen practice, not least because they open us to a spacious, immovable awareness, within which we can observe both our immediate experience and our lifelong conditioning: our urge to label whatever we encounter. Such moments are fostered by quiet sitting, but they can occur at any time and any place, be it a darkened zendo or the well-lit aisles of the Salvation Army.

July 3, 2008

Cooking with Dogen

*I*n *The Life and Letters of Tofu Roshi*, her gentle satire on Zen practice, the writer and photographer Susan Moon invents an eccentric Zen master who answers questions in the manner of "Dear Abby." When a young woman asks where she might go to meet cute guys, Tofu Roshi explains that if she's looking for psychologists, she should check out a Vipassana center, but if she's looking for poets and artists, she should do her cruising at a Tibetan monastery. If she fancies carpenters or cooks, she should head for the zendo.

Susan Ichi Su Moon is a long-time Zen practitioner, who knows whereof she speaks. Cooking and Zen practice have much in common, and over the centuries they have enjoyed an enduring relationship. Readers of a certain age may remember the *Tassajara Bread Book*, a popular cookbook in the days of the Whole Earth movement. Its author is Edward Espe Brown, an ordained Zen priest and one of the founders of the Greens restaurant in San Francisco. More recent cookbooks include Bettina Vitell's *A Taste of Heaven & Earth*, whose simple recipes generate complex flavors, and Seppo Edward Farrey's *Three Bowls*, which interleaves enticing recipes with vignettes of life in the zendo. Both Vitell and Farrey were head cooks at Dai Bosatsu Zendo, a Rinzai Zen monastery in the Catskills. Their books reflect their rigorous training.

The affinity between cooking and Zen may be traced, in part, to a classic text in the Zen tradition, Eihei Dogen's *Instruction for the Tenzo* (1237). Written by the founder of the Soto school of Zen, this text is at once a practical guide to the cook and a lucid exposition of an ethical perspective. At the practical level, Dogen advises the *tenzo* (head cook) of the monastery on such matters as the selection of lentils and the separation of rice from sand. At the philosophical level, he advocates a way of being and an attitude of mind. Faithfully held and thoroughly developed, this attitude will produce meals that embody the "three virtues" of mildness, cleanliness, and formality. And it will also advance the cook on the path of liberation.

Of the multiple components that make up Dogen's attitude to cooking, the most central is "sincerity," by which he means wholehearted attention to every last detail. "In the art of cooking," Dogen writes, "the essential consideration is to have a deeply sincere and respectful mind regardless of the fineness or coarseness of the materials." Rejecting conventional hierarchies, the tenzo will pay consistent attention to every task and every ingredient, however menial or exalted. "Do not be idle even for a moment," Dogen sternly advises. "Do not be careful about one thing and careless about another." Give as much attention to a "broth of wild grasses" as you would give to a "fine cream soup." The tenzo who implements this advice will learn "to turn things while being turned by things." He will realize "freedom from all discrimination."

For those of us who cook, Dogen's advice offers a challenge as well as an invitation. Can we give the chopping of onions the same attention as we give the measuring of rice? Can we show a lowly turnip the same respect as we show a delicate fillet of sole? If so, we will be cultivating a quality of mind and heart whose benefits extend well beyond the kitchen. And we might also cook a satisfying meal.

July 17, 2008

Springwater

A few weeks ago, I attended a retreat at the Springwater Center for Meditative Inquiry in Springwater, New York. Joining me were twenty-seven other retreatants, who had come from as far away as Germany, Sweden, Switzerland, and Nicaragua. For the better part of a week, we sat, walked, and worked in an atmosphere of silence, speaking only when necessary or during the afternoon discussions. In the words of Toni Packer, founder and director of the Springwater Center, we paused in our lives to "ask what is really going on" and "to feel the wholeness of what is here."

The Springwater Center is situated on a hillside amidst two hundred acres of open fields and woods. Its tall windows look out on the gentle hills of the Springwater Valley. Its simple but spacious facilities include a meditation hall, a dining room, accommodations for guests and staff, and even a modest library. Naturally lit, its interior spaces feel close to the outdoors. In the mornings we heard birdsong, in the evenings faint sounds from the town.

Toni Packer, who recently celebrated her eighty-first birthday, grew up in wartime Germany. She remembers the atmosphere of fear, the searchlights roaming the night sky. In her twenties she married an American and immigrated to the United States, settling in North Tonawanda. During the 1970s she studied Zen with Philip Kapleau, abbot of the Rochester Zen Center, where she became a senior student and Kapleau's designated successor. In 1984, however, she and a group of friends left Rochester to establish a center of their own. Dispensing with the liturgy, forms, and hierarchies of traditional Japanese Zen, they preserved the core of the practice, which for Toni Packer is one of pure listening and unmediated inquiry.

Pure listening, as defined by Toni, is listening without preconceptions. In her essay "Listening and Looking," she explains:

> There are different states of mind, and the state that is reacting most of the time when we are talking to each other is the state of memory. Our language comes out of memory, and we usually don't take time to think about the way we say things, let alone look carefully at what we are saying. We usually talk to each other and to ourselves in habitual, automatic ways.
>
> So we're asking, can there be talking and listening that are not solely governed by memory and habit, except for remembrance of the language and the various examples that are given? Can there be fresh speaking and fresh listening right now, undisturbed by what is known?

Described in this way, the "fresh listening" Toni advocates may resemble induced amnesia. But later on in her essay, she clarifies that point:

Can there be listening that does not abolish the personal past—that's impossible—but that sees it for what it is: memory, thought, image, and connected feelings and emotions? That collection is not what is actual right now! When there is open listening, the past is in abeyance.

As might be inferred from these excerpts, the practice of open listening fosters the practice of radical inquiry. "Here at Springwater," Toni has said, "we question everything." For Toni Packer that commitment meant questioning the Zen tradition itself, including its hallowed claims to authority. But whether she calls her practice "meditative inquiry," "the work of this moment," or something else, her spirit of listening and questioning goes to the heart of Zen.

If you would like to refresh your mind, while also examining your mental habits, you might wish to spend a few days at the Springwater Center, thirty-five miles north of Alfred. And unlike the retreatants from Europe, you won't have to cross the ocean to do it.

August 14, 2008

Innocence

Many years ago, I made a pilgrimage to the village of Inniskeen in Co. Monaghan, Ireland. The Irish poet Patrick Kavanagh (1904–1967) grew up on a small farm in Inniskeen and is buried in the village cemetery. After visiting his grave, which is marked by a simple wooden cross, I spoke with a local farmer, who remembered his illustrious neighbor."I knew Paddy," he told me. "His mother couldn't read or write. His father was a shoemaker. Paddy was not a good farmer—not good at all. He paid no heed to his fields."

Paddy Kavanagh paid no heed because his mind was elsewhere. He yearned to be in Dublin, where he could enjoy the bohemian life and pursue a literary career. At the age of thirty-five he finally left his farm for the big city, and within a decade he had become an internationally known poet. In "The Great Hunger" (1942), the poem that made him famous, he examined the spiritual and sexual deprivation of the Irish farmer. And in "Stony Grey Soil" he looked back in anger at his native ground, which had "clogged the feet of

[his] boyhood," "fed [him] on swinish food," and "burgled [his] bank of youth."

Yet Kavanagh also loved the "black hills" he had abandoned, and in "Innocence" he revisits the scenes of his childhood:

> They laughed at one I loved—
> The triangular hill that hung
> Under the Big Forth. They said
> That I was bounded by the whitethorn hedges
> Of the little farm and did not know the world.
> But I knew that love's doorway to life
> Is the same doorway everywhere.
>
> Ashamed of what I loved
> I flung her from me and called her a ditch
> Although she was smiling at me with violets.
>
> But now I am back in her briary arms
> The dew of an Indian Summer morning lies
> On bleached potato-stalks—
> What age am I?

Remembering his youth, he also recalls his innocence, which enabled him to take delight in the violets in the ditch and the dew on potato stalks. And in his closing lines, he embraces the environs he had scorned. "I cannot die," he declares, "Unless I walk outside these whitethorn hedges."

The quality of innocence so important to Kavanagh is also important in Zen practice, where it is known as "beginner's mind." A translation of the Japanese term *shoshin*, "beginner's mind" describes an openness to experience, unimpeded by preconceptions. In the book that introduced the term to the West, Shunryu Suzuki's *Zen Mind, Beginner's Mind*, Suzuki explains:

> *The goal of practice is always to keep our beginner's mind. ... This does not mean a closed mind, but actually an empty mind and a ready mind. If your mind is empty, it is ready for anything; it is open to everything. In the beginner's mind there are many possibilities; in the expert's mind there are few.*

Beginner's mind, in other words, is the mind before it is conditioned by knowledge, experience, and expectations.

Patrick Kavanagh sought to reclaim his innocence through the art of poetry. Zen practitioners cultivate beginner's mind through the discipline of meditation. But we needn't be poets or Zen monks to see the world afresh. We have only to quiet our minds and open our eyes.

August 28, 2008

Firewood and Ashes

*A*s I was driving on Route 21 the other day, I noticed a trailer full of firewood for sale. I was reminded of the winter, many years ago, when I burnt twenty face cords of firewood, most of it maple and beech.

I also recalled a statement, famous in Zen circles, by the founder of the Soto school of Zen, Eihei Dogen (1200–1250):

> *Firewood becomes ashes, it does not become wood again. Don't think that wood is first, ashes after. Your understanding must penetrate that although firewood is firewood, it has a before and after; that having this before, this after, it is free of these. ... Life is life, death is death and are each in their own place like winter and spring. Winter does not become spring, spring does not become winter.*

On first reading, this statement defies common sense. "Don't think that wood is first, ashes after"? Sometimes translated as "firewood does not turn into ashes," this sentence runs counter to our experience, as does Dogen's later assertion that "winter does not become spring, spring does not become winter." Obviously, winter *does* become spring, if rather late in Western New York.

Dogen's statement becomes more accessible if we remember that the image of firewood turning into ashes is a creation of the mind. It is a concept, a construction of thought. As such, it may help us to understand firewood—and to prepare for the process of burning, which will include the disposal of ashes. But it is still a concept, and though it may be useful, it can also impede our direct experience of firewood, right here and right now.

Direct experience, unmediated by conceptual thought, is the first concern of the Zen practitioner. In her commentary on Dogen's statement, Toni Packer addresses this aspect of the practice:

> *Zen Master Dogen once said, "Firewood does not turn into ashes." When I heard that the first time, I didn't know what he was talking about because obviously firewood turns into ashes. I mean, we've all experienced it. And the next time we had a campfire, I watched and observed, and the time quality fell away. It was just being there and there was no change from fire to ashes; it was just what was. Fire. And then sometimes it collapses, and there are some sparks, and it seems to turn black. But when you're really there, timelessly, it is not a process of time that is observed but presence: eternal, everlasting, without time.*

Packer goes on to say that once "you're just here … a response will come out of this intelligent or wise presence. One's response will be intelligent."

But doesn't Dogen also acknowledge that firewood has a "before and after"? Indeed he does, and surely an intelligent response to the burning of firewood must include a recognition of its past and its probable future. A stick of firewood was once a tree, and it will soon be ashes. To ignore—or attempt to ignore—those facts is to misconstrue the aim of Zen practice as merely "being present" or "living in the Now."

What Dogen and Toni Packer are urging is not simply living in the Now but cultivating a dual, or binocular, vision. Contemplating firewood, we are aware that it exists in time; it is turning into ashes even as we watch. But we are also experiencing what Zen calls its "suchness": its timeless presence, in all its brilliant vivacity. To see in both of these ways at once, to be present for the changing relative world while also being in touch with the timeless ground of being, is a primary aim of the Zen practitioner. And it is also a primary challenge of the practice.

September 11, 2008

Stability and Resilience

One afternoon, as I stood in a room in a Seattle hotel, I felt the building sway and the floor move beneath my feet. "What's going on?" I said aloud, before I realized what had happened.

The hotel had swayed because it was meant to. Like other skyscrapers, it was designed to sway by as much as a foot in a high wind. If that seems like a lot, we have only to consider the skyscraper presently under construction in Dubai. At its current height of 2,250 feet, the Burj Dubai is already the world's tallest man-made structure. Its pilings extend more than 150 feet into the ground. But when completed, its Sky Tower will sway as much as ten feet in the wind. A symbol of wealth and power, the Burj Dubai also exemplifies stability joined to resilience.

Although the human body is not a skyscraper, the posture of Zen meditation has much in common with the structure of tall buildings. Both require solidity below and flexibility above.

When we sit down to meditate, we first create a solid foundation. We sit on the first third of the cushion, letting our knees rest on the mat below. Crossing our legs in one of the "lotus" positions, we take care to elevate the pelvis above the knees. By so doing, we establish a triangular base of support, our two knees and our sitting bones becoming the three points of the triangle.

Having established that immovable base, we bend forward, then come up slowly, allowing the back to straighten itself. We push the crown of the head upward, stretching the spine. Rocking from side to side, we decrease this movement until the spine is vertical and aligned with the earth's gravitational force. Then we exhale, deeply and completely, as we relax into the posture of meditation. Although the upper body is motionless and upright, it is also flexible and light.

For Westerners, especially those accustomed to slouching in an armchair or sitting rigidly at a computer, this posture may initially feel uncomfortable. But with practice, it can become the most natural way of sitting, as well as the one most beneficial to the body and mind.

At the physical level, the posture of meditation promotes the free flow of air into and out of the lungs. More broadly, it permits the free flow of energy throughout the body. As the weight of the body settles into its center of gravity—the *hara*, or lower abdomen—our muscles relax, and our tensions lessen. Rather than resist the directional energies of gravitation, the body enjoys their support.

In tandem with the calming of the body, the posture of meditation also calms the mind. In Zen meditation, we sometimes count our exhalations or follow the movement of the breath into and out of our lungs. But even without these aids to concentration, the posture of meditation fosters clarity of mind. When the body is grounded, upright, and relaxed, the mind more easily sheds its fantasies and fears, its worries and incessant chatter.

Beyond these tangible benefits, the posture of meditation also engenders a more open attitude toward the world. In ordinary life, we often brace ourselves, physically and emotionally, against the "other," whether the other is threatening us or not. We defend what we call our "selves." By adopting the posture of meditation we cultivate a suppler and more receptive attitude toward the realities of our lives, however pleasant or unpleasant they may be. Like tall but resilient buildings, we sway in the wind.

September 25, 2008

The Cypress in the Garden

A few hours before Sarah Palin was to deliver her speech at the Republican National Convention, BBC correspondent Katty Kay observed that Ms. Palin seemed a little nervous.

"I guess we'd all be a bit nervous, wouldn't we?" replied anchorman Matt Frei, before moving on to another matter.

As it turned out, Governor Palin did not appear nervous at all. But I took note of the Kay-Frei exchange because it represents a conversational paradigm that has become conspicuous in recent years. It goes something like this:

"Nixon was a crooked politician."

"All politicians are crooked."

Or like this:

"I'm feeling sleepy tonight."

"You're always sleepy after dinner."

I could offer more examples, but perhaps the point is clear. In each instance a particular observation prompts a generalized reply. And the general statement trumps the particular. It no longer matters whether Sarah Palin was nervous or Nixon was crooked. It's as if the first speaker had noted a specific instance of a universal pattern, which the second speaker understands. Innocence meets experience, and the case is closed.

Whatever the origins of this paradigm, and whatever it might reflect about contemporary culture, to the Zen practitioner it represents the essential delusion that Zen warns us against, the dream from which we must awaken if we are to see things as they are.

Perhaps all politicians *are* crooked, but quite possibly some are not. But in this instance, as in the others, we will never know, because we have stopped inquiring. A general concept has taken the place of direct experience. A verbal absolute has masked the unprecedented, unrepeatable reality before us.

Because Zen practice is chiefly concerned with that reality, Zen is forever calling us back from the sphere of abstract thought to the concrete world in front of our noses. Only in the here and now, the Zen masters exhort us, can we live out the reality of our lives—or, as Thich Nhat Hanh puts it, "keep our appointment with life."

The Indian sage Bodhidharma is credited with bringing Zen Buddhism from India to China in the fifth century CE. In a well-known Zen koan, a student asks his teacher, the Ch'an master Joshu (778–897), why Bodhidharma came to China.

"The cypress in the garden," Joshu replies.

Like many a Zen koan, this appears to be a non sequitur. But it makes intuitive sense, once we realize that Joshu is hauling his student back from the ether of speculation to the world at hand. "Come home!" he might be saying. "Come home to where you are."

Joshu lived in a time very different from ours, but the story of his retort is worth remembering, if only because it offers an antidote to the malady I've been describing. "Stop and look!" it is telling us. And look into what you see.

October 9, 2008

Mountains and Rivers

"*B*efore I studied Zen," goes a famous Zen saying, "I saw mountains as mountains and rivers as rivers. When I had studied Zen for thirty years I no longer saw mountains as mountains and rivers as rivers. But now that I have finally mastered Zen, I once again see mountains as mountains and rivers as rivers."

The author of that saying is the poet and Ch'an master Ch'ing Yuan, who lived in the eighth century CE. However, his saying transcends its time and place, and it has long since entered Western culture. A version of it may be heard in the song "There Is a Mountain" by the Scottish folksinger Donovan.

Evoking the landscape of ancient China, Ch'ing Yuan's saying bears a foreign, romantic aura, but like many Zen proverbs it is also an eminently practical observation. It has less to do with objects seen than with a way of seeing. Ch'ing Yuan used mountains and rivers as examples because they were prominent presences in his daily life. But his saying becomes more accessible if we substitute presences that have become prominent—and troubling—in our own lives of late. I am thinking of American banks and, more broadly, of the global financial system.

To most of us, a bank is a bank. It is always there—an abiding presence that might well be a mountain, so central and established is its place in the community. We keep our money there—or rather, it keeps our money and our important papers, and we rely on it to do so. Although its rates, fees, and policies vary from year to year, its presence is as constant as it is secure. *You can take it to the bank*, we say, knowing exactly what we mean.

Yet, as Ch'ing Yuan discovered through thirty years of contemplation, mountains are not mountains, insofar as "mountains" denotes something that possesses a separate, intrinsic, and unchanging self. And, as many of us have recently discovered, banks are not as solid as they seem. Their names may remain the same, but their assets are constantly in flux. And however independent they may appear, they are components of an interdependent system, which is no more stable than our rapidly changing climate.

To recognize as much may be deeply distressing, but in the end it is liberating. No longer imprisoned by an illusion of solidity, we see, as Ch'ing Yuan did, the impermanence at the core of our existence. Having nothing solid to cling to, be it a mutual fund or a Treasury bond, we are released from clinging. And if we can extend this realization to all conditioned things, including our bodies, thoughts, and states of mind, we may experience what the Dalai Lama has called "the only true peace, the only true liberation."

Yet, as Ch'ing Yuan acknowledged in the third part of his saying, we live in the ordinary relative world, where mountains are mountains and banks are banks. Attachment to the illusion of permanence, financial or otherwise, can cause great suffering, but so can a lofty attachment to the insight of impermanence. That is why Zen teachings urge us to cultivate mindfulness in our everyday lives as well as in the zendo. By so doing, we maintain awareness of what Peter Matthiessen has called "the eternally rising and perishing reality of the world," even as we make our mortgage payments or reallocate our assets. And over time we come to rely on that immovable awareness, which isn't depressed when we're depressed or poor when we are poor. On the contrary, it is a refuge from temporal conditions, more dependable than any bank and more durable than any mountain.

October 30, 2008

Snobbery

*N*ot long ago, Dr. Emrys Westacott, Professor of Philosophy at Alfred University, gave a thought-provoking talk at the Bergren Forum. His subject was snobbery, which he defined in this way:

> *Believing without sufficient justification that you are superior to another person in certain respects because you are associated with some group that places you above them in a social hierarchy.*

Professor Westacott went on to explore this definition and to suggest that snobbery, so defined, may be unavoidable.

As definitions go, Professor Westacott's strikes me as sound and useful. At the same time, it points toward something deeper than social snobbery. From the standpoint of Zen teachings, it identifies a fundamental ignorance of reality and a root cause of human suffering. And it also implies a remedy, both for snobbery and its underlying causes.

To begin with, the snob, as here defined, assumes that he or she is a separate, unchanging self. Once a Harvard graduate, always a Harvard graduate. Once a star, always a star. Yet even a moment's reflection reveals that what one calls one's "self" is anything but permament or solid. Perhaps our temperaments remain constant from day to day—and decade to decade—but our circumstances and identities, social and personal, do not. Today's "superior" self may be something else tomorrow.

Beyond the impermanence of self, there is also the impermanence of one's ideas. Because an idea has occurred to us, we tend to believe it. And, more often than not, we identify with it, calling it "my" idea and defending it against detractors. But in reality the unquestioned ideas that cross our minds, including ideas about ourselves, are no more solid or permanent than the caws of crows or the sound of the UPS truck arriving in the driveway. To take them at face value, or assume that they reflect reality, is to court delusion.

Yet even if we acknowledge that both our selves and our attitudes are subject to change, we may persist in believing ourselves superior because, as Professor Westacott's definiton asserts, we are associated with a group that ranks high in the social order. But here again, that belief has feet of clay, because groups themselves are subject to change and revaluation. Yesterday's darling—Lehman Brothers, for example—can become tomorrow's pariah. In the current political climate, even "Harvard-educated" has become, in the minds of some, a political liability.

Given these realities, and given the unstable foundation on which social snobbery rests, it might seem odd that it continues to exist. Yet continue it does, bringing harm and folly in its wake. Is snobbery in fact unavoidable—a curse instrinsic to human nature?

Zen teachings would say no, because the very attribute that makes snobbery delusive—its insubstantial basis—also makes it vulnerable to dissolution. When practicing *zazen*, or seated meditation, we sit still and take note of whatever comes along, including the caws of crows and our notions of social superiority. *I drive a Lexus. He's still driving a Ford.* Bringing sustained awareness to notions of that kind, we begin to see them for what they are. We begin to see through them. And over time, as our practice strengthens and our awareness deepens, we may come to recognize our place in the web of life, where no one is solid or separate, superior or inferior, and all depend on one another.

November 6, 2008

Just Sitting

*J*undo Cohen, an American Zen priest who lives in Japan, often refers to the "tool kit" of meditative practices. Within the Japanese Zen tradition alone those practices include *susokkan* (counting out-breaths), *kin-hin* (walking meditation), *samu* (work practice), *oryoki* (formal meals), contemplation of koans, and *shikantaza* ("just sitting"). And that is to say nothing of the multitude of other methods, such as meditation on a text or repetition of a mantra, employed by the world's contemplative traditions.

Jundo himself practices shikantaza, which is also known as "objectless meditation." In most modes of meditation, the practitioner is instructed to focus on an object, tangible or intangible. In Zen practice that object is usually the flow of the breath, at least at the beginning of a sitting, but it can also be a koan, such as "Who hears the sound?" or "What was your original face before your parents were born?" In either case, we are enjoined to focus our attention, exclusively and singlemindedly, on a chosen object. By so doing, we enter the state of one-pointed concentration known as *samadhi*.

In practicing shikantaza, we dispense with all such methods. Insofar as we can, we do nothing but sit in awareness, noticing whatever comes along, including the sensations in our bodies, the coming and going of the breath, and the urge to be doing *something*—anything—but *just sitting*. Should we begin to slouch, we correct our posture, but apart from such corrections, we focus on nothing in particular. Instead, we cultivate a panoramic attention, opening our minds to all that is occurring, within and without. If thoughts cross our minds, we note them but do not pursue them. Nor do we attempt to analyze our thoughts or discern their emotional subtexts. We just sit.

Shikantaza is a composite word, made up of three discrete elements. *Shikan* is usually translated as "just" or "nothing but," and it connotes wholehearted attention. *Ta* is an intensifier, literally meaning "hit." *Za* means "to sit," or more broadly, "to sit together." Together these elements describe a practice of sitting in precise, continuous awareness.

Eido Shimano Roshi, a contemporary Zen master, explains the practice of shikantaza in this way:

> *This is zazen in which one neither seeks enlightenment nor rejects delusion. The purest zazen, it uses no devices as such; strictly speaking, there is no goal or method.* Shikan taza *practice is a manifestation of original enlightenment, and is at the same time a way toward its realization. ... Zazen is both something one* does *and something one essentially* is.

To sit without goals or methods is not so easy as it sounds. In a culture as competitive as ours, where *doing* rather than *being* is widely prized, such a practice presents an extraordinary challenge. But for all its rejection of goals, "just sitting" affords the diligent practitioneer uncommon rewards. In contrast to object-centered meditation, it trains us to include whatever we experience—and to let the things of this world reveal themselves, just as they are.

Shikantaza is best practiced under the guidance of a teacher, lest it become what Eido Roshi once called "shikan-waste of time." If you would like to explore the practice, I would recommend that you visit Jundo Cohen's Tree Leaf Zendo at www.treeleaf.org. There you will find detailed instructions, as well as a daily opportunity to sit with Jundo in shikantaza.

November 20, 2008

The Tow Rope

Three weeks ago, winter arrived in Western New York, catching some of us off guard. I was reminded of a poem by the twelfth-century Japanese poet Saigyo:

Neglectful, we've yet
to fix the towrope
to the sled—
and here they've piled up already,
the white snows of Koshi!

Tayumitsutsu
sori no hayao mo
tsukenaku ni
tsumorinikeru na
koshi no shirayuki

Perhaps as you read this poem, you were thinking of something you've left undone. For my own part, I'm thinking of a heavy wooden storm window, which I should have put up weeks ago. Across the centuries, it would seem, some things don't change.

Saigyo, however, was no ordinary homeowner. His real name was Sato Norikiyo, and he was born in 1118 in Kyoto to an aristocratic military family. Skilled in the martial arts, he became a private guard to a retired emperor. But at the age of twenty-two, Norikiyo renounced warfare to become a Buddhist monk. Living a solitary life, he traveled widely, writing lyric verse under the pen name Saigyo. Today he is one of the best-loved poets in Japan, second only to the haiku master Matsuo Basho (1644–1694), who took Saigyo's life's work as a model for his own.

The form of Saigyo's poem is the *waka*, the conventional form of Japanese court poetry. A five-line syllabic form with a pattern of 5-7-5-7-7, the waka resembles the haiku in the first three lines, but the addition of two extra lines allows for greater expansiveness and complexity. Often, as in Saigyo's poem, an abrupt shift of perspective occurs at the end of the third line. In Saigyo's mature poems, subjective and objective elements are held in balance, the former expressing the poet's feelings and the latter describing a natural phenomenon.

In this particular poem the first three lines report an oversight: Saigyo has neglected to fasten the towrope to the sled. Buddhist monks are supposed to be paying attention at all times and to be attuned to seasonal change. Perhaps Saigyo was too busy to bother with the towrope. Perhaps he forgot about it. In either case he realizes, here and now, that he has ignored the advent of winter and overlooked a necessary chore.

In the next two lines, the perspective shifts abruptly, as Saigyo turns our attention to the newfallen snow. Koshi is a coastal province, known for its heavy snows. Although Saigyo does not develop the scene, we can well imagine its natural beauty, which contrasts sharply with the human situation he has just described. If the human error is cause for consternation, the natural scene is cause for joy.

"Like many great Japanese poets," writes Burton Watson, a distinguished translator of Saigyo's poems, "he was not afraid of saying something very simple." Nor was he afraid to look at his human failing in the light of the impersonal natural world. In Saigyo's vision, human error and unforgiving nature are parts of the one body of reality. Open to both, he gives them equal standing. Engaged with both, he sees them as they are.

December 4, 2008

Being with Dying

"**S**now was general all over Ireland," writes James Joyce at the end of his short story "The Dead." In this celebrated story Gabriel Conroy, a middle-aged Dubliner, comes to terms with his own mortality. As often in Western literature, snow is a metaphor for death.

Today, what is general all over America—and indeed the world—is fear, whether its object be joblessness, a terrorist attack, or the more familiar specters of aging, sickness, and death. What have Zen teachings to say about fear? And what has Zen practice to offer?

One person who has confronted fear in general and the fear of death in particular is Joan Halifax Roshi, founder and Abbot of the Upaya Zen Center in Santa Fe, New Mexico. Trained as an anthropologist, Roshi Joan turned to Zen practice after the death of her grandmother. For the past four decades she has devoted her life to teaching Zen and caring for the dying.

In her new book, *Being with Dying* (Shambhala, 2008), Halifax presents the fruit of her life's work. Observing that the fear of death causes many of us to avoid, ignore, or otherwise deny the "only certainty of our lives," she reminds us that "to deny death is to deny life." And to embrace death can be the ultimate form of liberation:

> *The sooner we can embrace death, the more time we have to live completely, and to live in reality. Our acceptance of death influences not only the experience of dying but also the experience of living; life and death lie along the same continuum. One cannot—as so many of us try to do— lead life fully and struggle to keep the inevitable at bay.*

But how, exactly, are we to embrace death? To address our fear?

Halifax offer a wealth of "skillful means," including zazen, walking meditation, reflection on one's priorities, and the contemplation of nine perspectives on living and dying (*"The human life span is ever-decreasing; each breath brings us closer to death"*). But of her many strategems, two in particular stand out, the first of them a practical method, the second a matter of attitude.

Halifax calls her method "strong back, soft front." By this she means the posture of meditation, in which we first straighten, then relax, our backs, feeling the strength and stability of an upright spine. Having established that stability, we soften the front of our bodies, opening our lungs to the air and our minds to things as they are. We bring our presence, strengthened but softened, to whatever suffering we encounter.

Simple though it sounds, this practice can bring immediate calm. And over time, it can engender a profound shift of attitude :

To meet suffering and bear witness to it without collapsing or withdrawing into alienation, first we must stabilize the mind and make friends with it. Next, we open the mind to life—the whole of life, within and around us, seeing it clearly and unconditionally from that stable inner base. And then we fearlessly open our hearts to the world, welcoming it inside no matter how wretched or full of pain it might be. I've come to call this the "threefold transparency"—us being transparent to ourselves, the world's being transparent to us, and us being transparent to the world.

As Halifax readily acknowledges, this practice is anything but quick or easy. But with the necessary effort come eventual liberation and the capacity to be of genuine help to others. "It may take effort," she observes, "to return our mind to practice. And it usually takes effort to bring energy and commitment to everything we do. Effort at its very core means letting go of fear."

At a time when fear is as general as Joyce's snow, such a perspective is as worthy as it is rare.

December 18, 2008

108 Delusions

On New Year's Eve some people drink themselves silly. Others make improbable resolutions. In Japan, however, millions travel to Zen temples to listen to a heavy log strike the temple bell 108 times. Symbolically, the 108 strokes of the bell banish the 108 delusions to which the human mind is prone.

But why 108? Why not 107—or 10,001? In several spiritual traditions, the number 108 is thought to have numerological significance. Hindu deities have 108 names, and the recitation of their names is sometimes accompanied by the counting of 108 beads. Buddhist temples often have 108 steps, and Zen priests wear a string of 108 prayer beads on their wrists. In Homer's *Odyssey*, Odysseus's wife, Penelope, has 108 suitors, which Odysseus must dispatch before he and his missus can be reunited. In his book *Sailing Home*, the Zen priest Norman Fischer interprets this action as an allegory for the extinguishing of delusions.

Suggestive as such correspondences are, they are not enough to convince the Zen priest Anzan Hoshin Roshi, who argues that "108" is really the equivalent of "a lot." As he explains, "We say 108 because, well, that is a lot, isn't it? You can try to picture, say, three things, five things. At ten things it starts to get a little fuzzy. Try to picture 18 things, 37 things, *108 things*. Can't do it. So 108 means means measureless, numberless."

But what constitutes a delusion, and why does the human mind produce so many? In his classic satire *The Praise of Folly*, the Renaissance humanist Desiderius Erasmus contends that we human beings generate delusions to keep ourselves happy. To dramatize the point he enlists the goddess Folly, who delivers an ironic lecture in praise of herself. As Folly sees it, the more we fool ourselves about our looks, wit, learning, and the like, the happier we are. Therefore Folly, who makes this happiness possible, deserves our praise.

Zen takes another tack entirely. According to Zen teachings, delusion does not conduce to happiness. On the contrary, it is a primary cause of suffering. And the delusions that afflict us, however many their number, stem from a common root, which is sometimes called "a fundamental ignorance of reality," or more succinctly, egoistic delusion. Robert Aitken Roshi, an American Zen master, describes that core delusion in this way:

> *We desire permanent existence for ourselves and for our loved ones, and we desire to prove ourselves independent of others and superior to them. These desires conflict with the way things are: nothing abides, and everything and everyone depends on everything and everyone else. This conflict causes our anguish, and we project this anguish on those we meet.*

71

The *Heart Sutra*, chanted daily in Zen monasteries, calls these egocentric attitudes "upside-down views." And the second of the Four Great Vows, also chanted daily, describes delusions as "inexhaustible" and expresses the intent to "extinguish them all."

That is a tall order, and to some it may sound like a negative effort. But from the vantage point of Zen, the extinguishing of a delusion is also the opening of a "dharma gate": an opportunity to rid ourselves of self-deception, right our upside-down views, and live in harmony with the laws of reality. That is why the tolling of a temple bell on New Year's Eve, however solemn it may sound, is not a rite of mourning but truly a cause for celebration.

December 25, 2008

Ice Dams

If you own a home in Western New York, you may be familiar with ice dams. These pesky obstructions occur when heat escapes from a warm attic, melts the snow on the roof, and sends water trickling down to the cold eaves. There it freezes into mounds of ice, blocking the further flow of melting snow. Unless your roof is protected by an asphalt polymer membrane, the trapped water may find its way under the shingles and into the ceiling below.

Ice dams can cause no end of trouble. And so can their counterparts in the inner life, if we allow them to form and grow. In his article "The Mind's True Nature," the Tibetan poet and meditation master Dilgo Khyentse Rinpoche explains:

> *Water is soft and fluid, ice hard and sharp, so we cannot say that they are identical; but neither can we say that they are different, because ice is only solidified water, and water is only melted ice.*

The same applies to our perception of the world around us. To be attached to the reality of phenomena, to be tormented by attraction and repulsion, by pleasure and pain, gain and loss, fame and obscurity, praise and blame, creates a solidity in the mind. What we have to do, therefore, is to melt the ice of concepts into the living water of freedom within.

In this vivid analogy Dilgo Khyentse is describing dualistic thought: the process by which we habitually divide undifferentiated reality into concepts of this or that—into good and bad, beautiful and ugly, self and other, and so on. While necessary for survival, such concepts can all too easily freeze into rigid categories, to which we become attached, occluding our vision and blocking the stream of life.

But how do we "melt the ice of concepts into the living water of freedom within"? Franz Kafka, author of "The Metamorphosis" and other modern parables, once described a book as an "axe to the frozen sea within us." And Zen koans, which sometimes resemble Kafka's parables, can also serve that function. Contemplating a koan such as "Who hears the sound?" or "All things enter the One. But what does the One enter?" we are compelled to abandon conceptual thought, making room for direct, intuitive perception.

But there is also a gentler and more gradual method. It consists of sitting still and watching our sensations, thoughts, and mental states arise, take form, and eventually dissolve. Bringing relaxed attention to that inner stream, we may detect the counterpart of ice dams in our psyches: fixed ideas, inflexible beliefs, impermeable states of mind. *That's just the way I am,* we may be tempted to say. But should we continue to shine the lamp of mindfulness on those aggregates of thought and feeling, recognizing their impermanent and insubstantial nature, we may sense the beginning of a thaw. We may touch the ground of being—the common source of ice and water. And over time, we may taste the living water within.

January 15, 2009

Not-Knowing

*I*n November, 1972, I accompanied Dan and Lillyan Rhodes to the University of Rochester to hear a reading by the poet Gary Snyder. As some readers of this column may know, Daniel Rhodes was an internationally known potter, sculptor, and professor of ceramic art at Alfred University. He was also a longtime friend of Gary Snyder.

Of the poems I heard that evening, one in particular made a lasting impression:

PINE TREE TOPS

In the blue night
frost haze, the sky glows
with the moon
pine tree tops
bend snow-blue, fade
into sky, frost, starlight,
the creak of boots.
Rabbit tracks, deer tracks,
what do we know.

As he read the last line of his poem, Snyder stressed the word "we." What can *we* presume to know, he seemed to be asking, in the presence of the natural world's nocturnal beauty? His tone was one of awe, tempered by disdain for human presumption.

Gary Snyder's poem owes something to Ezra Pound, one of Snyder's poetic mentors, who admonished us to "pull down [our] vanity" and to "learn of the green world what can be [our] place." Snyder's lines also reflect his practical experience as logger and forest ranger, his empathic study of indigenous cultures, and his lifelong practice of Zen meditation.

In one well-known story from the lore of Zen, a monk sets out on a pilgrimage in his straw hat, robe, and sandals. Along the way he encounters a Zen master, who asks him where he's going. "Around on pilgrimage," the monk replies.

"What is the purpose of pilgrimage?" asks the master.

"I don't know," the monk confesses.

"Not knowing is the most intimate," replies the master.

That story is conventionally interpreted as an illustration of "beginner's mind." By not presuming to know where he is going, the monk is opening himself to whatever he encounters. Void of expectations and preconceptions, he can meet the world directly.

That interpretation is plausible enough, but Gudo Nishijima, a contemporary Zen master, has a different take on the story. In Nishijima's view, the monk's response acknowledges the limitations of his perceptions. To be sure, we usually know our immediate destinations. In relative terms, we know where we are going. In ultimate terms, however, we really have no idea where we're headed. By admitting as much, the monk remains in touch with ultimate reality, even as he lives in the relative world.

Thirty-six years ago, as I listened to Gary Snyder read "Pine Tree Tops," I did not know that Dan Rhodes would retire and leave Alfred the next year—or that he would die of a heart attack in Nevada in 1989, at the age of seventy-eight. Nor did I know that Gary Snyder, Beat poet and author of rugged lyric verse, would become an icon of the environmental movement, or that his progressive views on ecology, derived from the ancient principle of *ahimsa* ("non-harming"), would become moral imperatives in the early 21st century.

Gary Snyder is a man of wide erudition, with a deep respect for the natural and social sciences. In offering the teaching of not-knowing, he is not sanctioning an aggressive ignorance. Rather, he is urging an attitude of humility and reverence, lest we do further harm. Resonant at the time, his lines are even more urgent now.

January 29, 2009

Preferences

"April is the cruelest month," wrote T.S. Eliot, but here in Western New York, the month of February seems more deserving of that honor. And for the meditative practitioner, no month presents a sterner challenge. *Be here now?* You must be joking. I'd rather be in Sarasota. Or better yet, St. Lucia.

In the "Faith-Mind Sutra," Seng-ts'an, the Third Ancestor of the Zen tradition, offers this advice:

> *The Great Way is not difficult*
> *for those not attached to preferences.*
> *When neither love nor hate arises,*
> *all is clear and undisguised.*
> *Separate by the smallest amount, however,*
> *and you are as far from it as heaven is from earth.*

To follow the Great Way—the path of liberation from conditioned suffering—is to set aside our habitual preferences. Summer over winter, for instance. Or, in winter, St. Lucia over Western New York.

That may sound like being numb or in denial, but in its context Seng-ts'an's meaning is quite the opposite. What he is urging is an openness to whatever we encounter, be it sun-drenched beaches or sub-zero temperatures, cloudless tropical skies or a Buffalo winter. Putting our preferences in abeyance, we fully experience our environs.

Beyond that, Seng-ts'an is enjoining us to recognize that by preferring one thing over another, we separate ourselves from the world we live in. We identify with our preferences, fashioning an "I" that dislikes cold weather, that prefers sand and sun over ice and snow. If what we prefer is presently available, we like it and want more of it—and want it to last forever. But if it's not, we stand apart, resisting what is present and complaining of our lot. On a really frigid day, we blame the cold for being cold, the winter for being winter.

Such responses are not to be suppressed. Their roots lie in generations of conditioning and in social forces well beyond our control. At the same time, what has been learned can be unlearned, and what is causing us suffering can be diminished, not by willful self-denial or efforts at self-improvement but by patient meditative inquiry. In her essay "Consciousness, Attention, and Awareness," the Zen-trained teacher Toni Packer puts it this way:

> Sometimes people say, "I ought to drop this habit, but I can't." No one is asking us to drop anything. How can we drop things when we are in our customary thinking and suffering mode? We can drop a bowl of cereal, but our habitual reactions need to be seen thoroughly as they are taking place. When there is awareness, a reaction that is seen and understood to be a hindrance diminishes on its

own. It may take a lot of repeated suffering, but a mo-
ment comes when the energy of seeing takes the place of
the habit. That is all. Seeing is empty of self. The root of
habit too is empty.

Rather than struggle to drop our habitual reactions, we cultivate awareness of those reactions and allow them to change
in their own time.

If you would like to explore this practice, you might wish
to take a meditative walk on a cold winter day. As you set
out, bring your awareness to your body—to your feet as they
slog through the snow, your arms as they rhythmically swing,
your face as it meets the cold. Open your eyes to the landscape, your ears to the sounds of winter. Then bring your
awareness to your resistance: to the concepts and judgments
that cross your mind. Pay particular attention to your likes
and dislikes, your comforts and discomforts. Continue this
practice through the month of February, and see what becomes of your aversions.

February 12, 2009

Attention, Attention, Attention!

*F*or the student of Zen, the world provides a multitude of teachers. From rooted, resilient trees we can learn the posture of meditation. From the birds we can learn directness of response. And from other people, particularly those whose trades have taught them to live in the present, we can learn a fundamental principle of Zen practice.

Thirty-five years ago, my first wife and I were living in a rundown farmhouse on Elm Valley Road. Asphalt-shingled and lacking insulation, our house was drafty and expensive to heat. To make ends meet, we installed three woodstoves, which we fed with maple, beech, and ash throughout the winter. Most of the firewood came from our woodlot across the road. I bought a 14" Homelite chainsaw at Carter Hardware, and though I'd had no experience with such a machine, I learned how to use it.

Or at least I thought I did, until I met Howard "Chainsaw" Chilson, my neighbor from down the road. Driving his little Ford tractor past our house, as he often did, Howard spotted me cutting wood and stopped to help, offering some pointers along the way. He showed me how to adjust the chain and how to trim branches without jamming the bar. Most important, he exhorted me to pay attention—full attention—to whatever I was doing. Although I did not quite realize it at the time, my eyes, limbs, and indeed my life depended on it.

Howard had served as an MP in the Second World War. A rugged, lanky man with a bone-crushing handshake, he proudly claimed to be "one-quarter Indian"—Cherokee, as I recall. His own chainsaw was a green, 20" Poulan, which looked as weathered as its owner. But in Howard's hands it might have been a scalpel, so prodigious was his skill.

Howard's prized tool had also earned him his name. As he told the story, he was refused service at a local bar, having come in drunk. Disappointed with this lack of courtesy, Howard went out to his truck and returned with his chainsaw. "Either serve me," he bellowed, "or I'll cut your bar down!." Although he did not make good on his threat, he was known ever after as Chainsaw Chilson.

Howard could be moody, but he was an amiable companion, and we spent many productive hours in the woods, cutting and hauling enough wood to heat two houses. Although he'd had little formal education, Howard had a woodsman's expertise, which he generously shared, and a keen observant eye, which he often turned in my direction. In three summers of working together we never had an accident or sustained even a minor injury, thanks mainly to Howard's vigilance. Although he called me "Boss," it was he who kept us both from harm. And though he chided me for wearing something so unmanly as ear protectors ("ear muffs,"he called them), he provided protection of his own, bringing my sometimes wandering mind back to the work at hand.

That is exactly what a good Zen teacher does, and though Chainsaw Chilson, who passed away in 1991, had probably never heard of Zen meditation, he had something in common with the long lineage of Zen teachers. "Will you please write some maxims of the highest wisdom?" a man asked Ikkyu, a fifteenth-century Zen master. "Attention, attention, attention!" Ikkyu wrote. And in a well-known poem, Layman P'ang, a C'han master of the eighth century, trains his own attention on ordinary labor. "Who cares about wealth and honor?" he writes, "Even the poorest thing shines. / My miraculous power and spiritual activity: / drawing water and carrying wood."

February 26, 2009

As Surely as One's Shadow

*A*s I look out our kitchen window, the most prominent presence in my field of vision is the fifty-year-
old pin oak tree in our backyard. Embedded in its
trunk, halfway up, is a red metal hook, which the bark has
nearly concealed. Running up and down from the hook is a
long, deep crack.

Twenty years ago, I screwed that six-inch bike hook
into the trunk. At the time, I owned no clothes dryer, and it
occurred to me that I might run a clothesline between the
house and the tree. My notion was innocent enough, and, by
today's ecological standards, admirably green. What did not
occur to me is that I might injure the tree.

As injuries go, the one I inflicted is less than catastrophic.
Over the past two decades, the oak tree has thrived, and now
it towers above our house, providing shade in the summer
and a year-round habitat for birds and other creatures. It is,
in fact, in vigorous health, as shown by the volume of acorns
it dumps on our deck, the piles of leaves it deposits in our
gutters.

Yet that red hook remains, as does the ugly scar it caused. And together they illustrate the principle of cause and effect, which in Zen teachings is known as *karma*. In popular culture, that word carries mystical associations, conjuring a chain of causation that extends well beyond the boundaries of this life. But the root meaning of "karma" is simply "action," and, as used in Zen, it usually means just that. *This is because that is.* Our words and deeds have consequences. In the words of Zen master Thich Nhat Hanh, what we say and do creates "our continuation, whether we want it to be so or not."

To those of a reflective disposition, that is hardly news. Live long enough, and you will observe the long-term effects of even the most casual compliment, insult, reassurance, or rebuke. And that is to say nothing of our major actions, personal, social, and political—actions whose effects may ramify for generations. But in Zen teachings, as in the law, it is not only words and deeds that matter. So do the thoughts that gave rise to the words and deeds.

"Mind," we are told in the first verse of the *Dhammapada*, a fundamental text in the Zen tradition, "is the forerunner of action. / All deeds are led by mind, created by mind. / If one speaks or acts with a corrupt mind, suffering will follow, / As the cart follows the hoof of the ox." Conversely, if one "speaks or acts with a serene mind / Happiness will follow, / As surely as one's shadow."

Taken seriously, these lines have serious implications. We are responsible, they imply, for our thoughts and states of mind as well as our words and deeds. And we are also responsible for cultivating a "serene" mind, which is to say, a mind that looks deeply, sees clearly, and causes as little harm as possible.

As I look out our kitchen window in the early mornings, I am sometimes reminded of those admonitions.

March 12, 2009

The Mother Road

"The present contains the past," writes the Vietnamese Zen master Thich Nhat Hanh. "The materials of the past which make up the present become clear when they express themselves in the present."

A few months ago, I was reminded of Thich Nhat Hanh's words, as I sat in the main room of Flint's Auto Center in Almond, waiting for a new battery to be installed in my wife's car.

All around me, the present made its presence felt. As I surveyed the room, I noticed the tall stacks of virgin tires, the bright green batteries on the racks, the factory-fresh fan belts hanging near the ceiling. The phone rang, and someone left a message. Moments later, a hurried young man came in, asking if his car could be inspected that very day. Over the next quarter of an hour, three more customers arrived.

Yet amidst these signs of a thriving business, the past was also expressing itself. High on a shelf lay a vintage copper washboard and a stash of antique toys—a model airplane, a red bus, a metal chicken. On the shelf below stood well-worn cans bearing their famous names: *Boraxo, Prince Albert, Gilley's Beer.* Not far away were a Ranger fire extinguisher, a Woodman Bee Smoker, and one of John Flint's family heir-looms: a manual, cast-iron meat grinder, with which many a sandwich was prepared.

Beyond these evocative relics, what caught and held my attention were the gas-pump signs on the far wall. *Esso. White Star. Sky Chief. Fire Chief. Sinclair Dino.* Some readers of this column may know that Fire Chief referred to Texaco Fire Chief, a gasoline with an octane high enough to be used in fire engines. A popular radio show of the thirties featured Ed Wynn, the Texaco Fire Chief. "Sinclair Dino" referred to the company's hugely successful logo, a benign brontosaurus. As part of its imaginative promotion, Sinclair put out, in 1935, a dinosaur stamp album that could be filled only with Dino stamps issued at Sinclair stations. That the gas-guzzling cars of ensuing decades might themselves become dinosaurs was not on anyone's mind.

"The car used to be greatly admired and desired," remarks John Casesa, a leading automotive analyst, "but now some people see it as something that is not good for us, like tobacco. ... The sound of a gas engine, the V8—those are going to be increasingly rare commodities. Maybe we're going to have to give up that seven-tenths of a second from zero to sixty."

Maybe so. But as Thich Nhat Hanh often says, the present is made up of the past, and we can learn from contemplating the materials of a bygone era. "If we observe these materials deeply," he suggests, "we can arrive at a new understanding of them. That is called 'looking again at something old in order to learn something new'."

If you would like to reflect on America's long romance with the car and the culture of the open road, while also having your car or truck reliably serviced, you need look no further than Flint's Auto Center in Almond, New York. And while you're there, don't overlook the rows of original license plates that line the walls or the roadsign that reads *New Mexico, Route 66.* Spanning the 2,448 miles from Chicago to Los Angeles and celebrated in Bobby Troup's famous song, Route 66 was the trail of choice for migrants, dreamers, the Dust Bowl poor, and all those headed west. Some called it the Main Street of America. John Steinbeck called it the Mother Road.

March 26, 2009

A Single Gentian

*T*he Burren is a limestone plateau in County Clare, Ireland. Occupying more than a hundred square miles, it is one of the quietest places on earth, and its gray expanse has often been likened to a lunar landscape. Yet it also hosts more than six hundred varieties of flowering plants, which thrive in reflected light.

Here is a poem set in the Burren. Its author is Michael Longley, one of Ireland's finest poets and a lifelong resident of Belfast:

AT POLL SALACH
Easter Sunday, 1998

While I was looking for Easter snow on the hills
You showed me, like a concentration of violets
Or a fragment from some future unimagined sky
A single spring gentian shivering at our feet.

Poll Salach (pronounced *pole sol-ock*) means "dirty pool" in the Irish language. Poll Salach is situated in the northwest region of the Burren, where the limestone pavement runs into the sea. Despite its name, it is an austere and beautiful site.

The narrator of this poem is walking at Poll Salach, and with a little help from an unnamed companion, he discovers a spring gentian (*Gentian verna*), a solitary flower. Its five petals are a bright blue, and to the poet the flower resembles a "concentration of violets." At its center is a pure white throat. According to Irish folklore, to pick a spring gentian is to precipitate an early death. To bring one indoors will cause your house to be struck by lightning.

It is significant that the narrator of this poem was looking for one thing—Easter snow—and discovered another. As the Zen teacher Toni Packer has remarked, most of the time we are looking *for* something, but we can also cultivate pure looking, or looking for its own sake. In that way we open ourselves to what is present in the here and now.

Something of that kind happens to the narrator of "Poll Salach," though he is also thinking of the future. For him, the blue of the gentian conjures a "future unimagined sky," which is to say, a future that has yet to be envisioned, much less determined.

Michael Longley wrote "At Poll Salach" on Easter Sunday, 1998, two days after the Good Friday Agreement was signed in Belfast. The Good Friday Agreement signaled an end to the sectarian violence in Northern Ireland, which had claimed more than 3,000 lives. In the ensuing decade, paramilitaries on both sides of the conflict have relinquished fighting and put their faith in peace and reconciliation.

Last month that truce was threatened, when dissidents from the Irish Republican Army killed two unarmed British soldiers and a member of the Police Service of Northern Ireland, which is now composed of Catholics as well as Protestants. This time, however, the leaders of the once-warring sides united in condemning the atrocities and renewing their commitment to peace.

It remains to be seen whether that peace will hold. Edna Longley, Michael's wife and a prominent literary critic, has described the "shivering" gentian in her husband's poem as a "tentative floral image," which indeed it is. But it is also an image of hope, as potent in its way as the lilies of Easter Sunday.

April 9, 2009

The Thoughtless People

When my son, Alexander, was a child we often took walks around the village of Alfred on Sunday mornings. We had no agenda, other than to spend some time together and to explore our surroundings.

Being closer to the ground, Alexander sometimes noticed things that I overlooked. On one April morning, he spotted two crumpled plastic cups near Seidlin Hall. They reeked of stale beer. "Who put those there?" he asked.

"Thoughtless people," I replied.

A few weeks later, Alexander noticed some crushed soda cans in the Kanakadea Creek. "It must have been the Thoughtless People," he concluded. In his imagination, I surmised, the Thoughtless People had become a band of feckless nincompoops, who roved the streets of Alfred, New York, dropping refuse wherever they went.

Perhaps he was not far wrong. But in retrospect, I wonder whether my response to his question, however fatherly, was all that wise. At best, it was incomplete.

If there are Thoughtless People, there must also be Thoughtful People. The one implies the other. In my eagerness to teach a moral lesson, I had created a moral duality, from which my six-year-old son had fashioned an image of his own. In the technical language of philosophy, he had reified an abstraction. On the one side were the Thoughtless People, on the other the Thoughtful People. People who know better. People like ourselves.

Twelve years earlier, Joni Mitchell had done something similar in her song "Big Yellow Taxi." In that 1970 song Joni complained that an unspecified "they" had "paved paradise / and put in a parking lot." In a subsequent verse she admonished farmers to "put away that D.D.T." before it destroyed "the birds and the bees." On the one side of her moral polarity stood avaricious developers and pesticide-wielding farmers; on the other, the trees, birds, and bees—and virtuous enviromentalists like herself.

To be sure, such polarities serve a practical purpose. Certain people, and certain aggregates of people, tend to be greedy, thoughtless, and destructive. For the sake of ethical clarity, if not also for the common good, it is sometimes necessary to call a spade a spade: to identify such people and such groups, using the familiar language of dualistic thought.

The danger lies in reifying our abstractions, which is to say, in mistaking our moral categories for reality. And one of the benefits of meditation, regularly practiced, is to reveal to us that in the flux of undifferentiated reality, prior to the imposition of moral concepts, there are no Thoughtless or Thoughtful People. There are only actions, our own and others'—actions that have an impact on the web of life.

In his book *Coming to Our Senses*, Jon Kabat-Zinn puts it this way:

> *In any given moment, we are either practicing mindfulness or, de facto, we are practicing mindlessness. When framed in this way, we might want to take more responsibility for how we meet the world, inwardly and outwardly in any and every moment—especially given that there just aren't any "in-between" moments in our lives.*

Viewing the past in this perspective, we can recognize and regret our thoughtless and destructive actions without being held forever in their thrall. But by the same token, we can no longer take refuge in images of ourselves as Thoughtful—or Mindful—People. At any future moment, our words and deeds may be thoughtful or thoughtless, mindful or mindless. And much will depend on the difference.

April 23, 2009

A Sense of Ceremony

*I*n the Rinzai Zen tradition, the first interview between student and teacher is an auspicious formal occasion. The required attire includes not only a robe but also the white booties known as *tabi*, which cover the feet and ankles. Tabi are fastened with hooks and eyes located on the inside of the ankle. For Westerners they are difficult to manage, even on the best of days.

On the morning of my own first interview with Jiro Osho Fernando Afable at Dai Bosatsu Zendo, a formal Rinzai monastery, I forgot all about my tabi. They were nestled like sleeping rabbits in the sleeves of my robe. As I prepared to leave for my interview, a senior monk noticed my oversight. He gestured sternly toward my feet, and I took his point.

Unfortunately, there are no chairs in a Japanese zendo. Rather than hunker on a cushion, I stood on one foot, then the other, as I struggled to put on my tabi. At one point, I hopped; at another, I nearly fell over. It must have taken me three minutes to marshal my partially hooked tabi into a semblance of order. Meanwhile, the senior monk was summoning every bit of his Zen discipline to keep a straight face. I suspect that he told the story to his fellow monks later on.

Embarrassing though it was, my awkwardness was not unusual. Ceremonial forms abound in Japanese Zen, and to the uninitiated Westerner they often feel as alien as they are compelling. From the relatively simple protocol known as *ju-kai*, in which a lay practitioner "receives the precepts," to the high theater of *shitsugo*, in which a seasoned priest receives the title of *roshi*, public ceremonies acknowledge the practitioner's deepening insight. And even on ordinary days, when nothing special is being recognized, celebrated, or commemorated, a sense of ceremony permeates the zendo. It can be seen in the bows and heard in the bells. It can be smelled in the incense. For the Western lay practitioner, this pervasive atmosphere of ceremony presents a challenge to the skeptical mind as well as the reluctant body. How much Asian ceremony should be included in a Western lay practice? How much is essential?

In addressing those questions, it is important to remember that Asian ceremonial forms, as used in Zen, exist primarily to support the practice of mindfulness. Pressing the palms together and bowing to one's teacher, for example, is a way of expressing gratitude and respect. But it is also a way of *knowing* that one is expressing gratitude and respect and a way of cultivating those states of mind. For those prepared to embrace them, the bows, chants, prostrations, and other elements of traditional Zen can become as integral to the practice as awareness of breath and posture.

For those who are not, however, there is another way of integrating a sense of ceremony into one's daily life. It is well described by Brother Joseph Keenan (1932–1999), who taught religion at La Salle University and was also a master of the Japanese tea ceremony:

> *The making of a bed, the folding of laundry, walking down stairs, driving a car to work—instead of racing through these actions with the mind-set of simply getting them done, savor them as present moments which contain hidden riches, and do them in the most beautiful way. Do them not from egotistical motives of self-fulfillment, but rather as gifts to the world that express to those you meet that you really want to present the best to them. In this approach to life even in today's world ... the niggling details of the daily grind can become moments of joy, moments filled with sweet nectar to be savored rather than tension-filled tasks. With this sort of attention to mundane actions, you can open yourself and others to a greater awareness of what is around you in the here and now.*

Although Brother Keenan is speaking of the tea ceremony, his description applies equally to a committed lay practice. In such a practice, each mundane task becomes an occasion for ceremonial regard. Each is an end in itself, not a means to a practical end. Each is an act of giving.

May 7, 2009

What Is This?

*I*f you have been reading this column for a while, you may remember Imre, the rambunctious three-year-old whom I taught to sit still. As his reward, he received a matchbox car.

Imre is now four, and he recently learned the word *forsythia*. At the time, we were examining the forsythia bush in our front yard. Its buds were green and about to turn yellow. "Can you say *forsythia*?" I asked.

Imre could not. So I broke the word into syllables, giving special emphasis to the second, which is difficult to pronounce. *For-SITH-ee-uh.* Imre practiced the word several times and finally got it—more or less. He seemed pleased with his achievement, though his newly acquired word could not compete with the word *stinky*, which he relished saying, over and over.

The forsythia plant is named after William Forsyth (1737–1804), a Scottish botanist and a founding member of the Royal Horticultural Society. Had it been named after William's great-grandson, Joseph Forsyth Johnson (1840–

1906), the famous gardener and landscape architect, it would been much easier for Imre to pronounce. But perhaps it deserves the more difficult name, being as it is a foreign import.

The forsythia is a genus in the olive family, with eleven species, all but one of them native to eastern Asia. Forsythia is an integral component of Chinese medicine and is sometimes used in Chinese cooking. In Korea, a stringed instrument called the *ajaeng* is played with a stick of forsythia wood. The stick is scraped across the strings, producing a deep and raspy sound.

Given its exotic origins, the forsythia might be regarded in Western New York as a prized plant, worthy of infinite care. As it happens, it is more often viewed as a common shrub, whose chief function is to announce, in bright yellow hues, the end of another winter. By some, the forsythia is seen as a nuisance, requiring frequent pruning if it is not to become a monster. To a four-year-old child, a forsythia bush is something new and even exciting. But is it possible for conditioned adults like ourselves to see it afresh?

According to one school of Zen thinking, the name itself presents an obstacle. In a four-line poem fundamental to the Zen tradition, the First Zen Ancestor, Bodhidharma, describes Zen as a practice of "direct seeing, not dependent on words and letters." Following Bodhidharma's lead, Zen teachers sometimes view language with suspicion and regard words as impediments to fresh seeing. The word forsythia is one thing, the shrub another. Proud of knowing the name, we may fail to see the object at all.

That point is well taken, but knowing the name of a plant or tree can sometimes help us to notice it. And beyond that, the name can provide access to its "suchness"—its unique and transient presence.

If you would like to experience this for yourself, sit in a comfortable, upright position, following your breathing. Choose an object in your surroundings, and while looking at that object, contemplate its name. Repeat the word slowly, listening to its consonants and vowels. As you continue to intone the name, notice how its meaning gradually dissolves, leaving a succession of syllables or merely a gauze of sound. At that point, ask the question "What is this?" Let the question resonate in silence. Then ask it again, and yet again, and see where it leads you.

First propounded by the fourteenth-century Zen master Bassui Tokushō, the question "What is this?" is sometimes followed, in Zen practice, with the statement "I don't know." Practiced with diligence, Bassui's koan can reveal the limitations of our knowledge and our language. It can remove our mental cataracts and restore our sense of wonder. And it can refresh a world "sicklied o'er," as Hamlet put it, "with the pale cast of thought."

May 21, 2009

"entrancements"!

Stepping Stones

I n his memoir "Something to Write Home About" the poet Seamus Heaney recalls an experience from his rural childhood in Northern Ireland. Near his parents' farm in Co. Derry, there was a ford in the River Moyola. A trail of stepping stones led from one bank to the other. Venturing into the river, "from one stepping stone to the next," he felt a sense of security mixed with a sense of daring:

vs

> Suddenly you were on your own. You were giddy and rooted to the spot at one and the same time. Your body stood stock still, like a milestone or a boundary mark, but your head would be light and swimming from the rush of the river at your feet and the big stately movement of the clouds in the sky above your head.

Looking back at this experience, Heaney sees it as a metaphor for the capacity of human beings "to be attracted at one and the same time to the security of what is intimately known and the challenges and entrancements of what is beyond us." For the poet Heaney, the experience is also a meta-phor for a good poem, which "allows you to have your feet on the ground and your head in the air simultaneously."

Seamus Heaney is not a Zen practitioner, though his po-ems often have a contemplative character. But his experience of standing "stock still" in the middle of a river, with the cur-rent flowing past him and the clouds moving above his head, has something in common with the practice of Zen medita-tion.

In practicing *zazen,* or seated meditation, we assume a posture that resembles a pyramid. Using the meditation cushion as a wedge, we keep our knees on the mat below, forming a triangle with our sitting bones. Leaning forward, then straightening up, we allow the spine to assume its nat-ural curvature, erect but resilient. Exhaling fully in this po-sition, we let our weight and our awareness drop into the lower abdomen. As we settle into stillness, we feel aligned and firmly grounded. To heighten our awareness of our sta-ble posture, Thich Nhat Hanh suggests we silently recite the verses, "Breathing in, I see myself as a mountain. / Breathing out, I feel solid."

Yet if the posture of meditation engenders feelings of so-lidity, it also fosters openness to experience. Because we are sitting still, we become more sensitive to movement within and around us, be it the flow of breath or the buzz of a fly at the window. Because our posture promotes relaxed alertness, we can observe the thoughts that cross our minds, as though they were clouds in the sky. And because we are resting in awareness, we can recognize those mental habits—those re-current memories, fantasies, and expectations—that leave little room for anything more productive. Merely by bringing awareness to that mental traffic, we may cause it to diminish, clearing a space for creative thought.

In December, 1995, Seamus Heaney traveled to Stockholm to receive the Nobel Prize for Literature. In "Crediting Poetry," his Nobel Lecture, he reflected on his "journey into the wideness of language, a journey where each point of arrival—whether in one's poetry or one's life—turned out to be a stepping stone rather than a destination." For the meditative practitioner, whose aim is the deepening of awareness, wisdom, and compassion, the journey may be very different, but the underlying pattern is much the same. Successive acts of attention, made possible by the practitioner's stable base, open the ego-centered self to a more expansive reality, be it the wideness of language or the ocean of human suffering. On the long path toward compassionate understanding, each moment fully realized becomes a stepping stone, each step a fresh arrival.

Thoughts = clouds in the sky.

June 4, 2009

Breathing in, I see myself as a mountain.
Breathing out, I feel solid.

Thich Nhat Hanh

Life is a long path to compassionate understanding.

Each moment fully realized = a stepping stone and an arrival.

Seven Words

A few years ago, the American poet Jane Hirshfield was invited to define Zen practice in seven words. As a young woman Hirshfield spent eight years in full-time Zen training, three of them in a Zen monastery. "That experience," she has said, "and its continuing life in my life underlie everything I have done since." How might Hirshfield's deep, experiential understanding of Zen, which she views as a path parallel to that of poetry, be articulated in seven words?

To appreciate the daunting nature of Hirshfield's task, even for a writer of her abilities, please take a minute to try it yourself. Choose something you know well and have known for a long time. Then try to define your subject in seven words. An anonymous Roman writer, who chose the brevity of life as his or her subject, wrote the motto *ut hora sic vita*, which became, in English, "As an hour, so is this life." That was a feat of rhetoric as well as a distillation of insight. And it illustrates, not incidentally, that in comparison with Latin, English is a rather wordy language. To say anything of substance in seven English words is itself a worthy challenge.

For the writer who would define Zen, three additional obstacles present themselves. Considered singly, they demonstrate the limitations of any proposed definition. Taken together, they illustrate the paradoxical nature of Zen practice.

To begin with, the tradition known collectively as Zen has changed dramatically over the centuries. Zen is thought to have originated in the sixth century CE, when the Indian monk Bodhidharma, the First Ancestor of Zen, brought the practice of *dhyana*, or meditation, to China. There it mingled with Confucian and Taoist elements and became known as *Chan*, the Chinese word for *dhyana*. When Chan arrived in Japan four centuries later, it became *Zen*, the Japanese word for Chan, and it acquired a distinctively Japanese character. In its subsequent migrations through Asia and, more recently, Europe and North America, Zen has continued to adapt to its changing cultural contexts. How can a practice so fluid and protean be defined in seven words?

A second obstacle lies in the interdependent relationship of Zen to other fields of human endeavor. In its rites and rituals, formal Zen resembles a religious order, though it's also been called the "religion before religions." As a rigorous physical discipline, requiring one-pointed concentration, it has something in common with the martial arts. As a form of inquiry that aims to relieve human suffering, it shares common cause with psychology, particularly cognitive therapy. And as an aesthetic, embodying principles of harmony, simplicity, and directness, it has influenced artistic pursuits as diverse as architecture, painting, tea-drinking, and landscape

107

gardening. How can a practice so interconnected with others be isolated in a simple definition?

And last, though Zen can be readily identified by a noun, it is not really an entity. It is not a solid thing. Rather, it is an activity—a continuing practice of mindfulness. As Eido Shimano Roshi reminds us, "Zazen is both something one *does*—sitting cross-legged, with proper posture and correct breathing—and something one essentially *is*. To emphasize one aspect at the expense of the other is to misunderstand this subtle and profound practice." But whether one emphasizes *does* or *is*, both are verbs; both point toward an evolving practice, not a static form. How can a definition, which assumes some degree of stability, be applied to a practice that is inherently vibrant, unpredictable, and ever-changing?

Jane Hirshfield found her own way. "Zen pretty much comes down to three things," she wrote. "Everything changes; everything is connected; pay attention."

June 18, 2009

Every thing changes;
every thing is connected;
pay attention.
                    Jane Hirshfield

Me and Mu

*I*n New York State you can own a Personalized License Plate, better known as a vanity plate, for $43.00. To retain your plate you will need to pay an annual fee of $25.50. Depending on your viewpoint, that is a lot or not much to pay for the privilege of having your name—or that of your trade, your passion, or your favorite sport—emblazoned on your car.

As I was driving on the New York State Thruway the other day, I came upon the ultimate vanity plate. Pulling into a rest stop, I noticed the out-of-state license plate on a sporty silver car. In bold black letters, it proclaimed its owner's first concern:

ME

On either side of these letters were several inches of white space, which gave further prominence to this one, all-important word.

It's common to hear the word "me" in conversation, but it was striking to find that word isolated on a license plate. I was reminded of a poem by my one-time mentor, the

Maine poet Philip Booth (1925–2007). Entitled "Marches," the poem is an exploration of seasonal change and human mortality.

In the first four stanzas the narrator reflects on the advent of spring, imagines the young "wading the surf, getting wasted, pretending / they cannot die," and envisions "thousands of death-needles" being passed, leaving "hundreds of / children... born with systems in no way immune." In the last two stanzas, he reflects on the imminence of death in everyday life, especially life on the highway:

> And millions of the rest of us, self-righteous
> in the perfect democracy of backcountry roads, freeways,
> and interstates, pass each other at life-span speeds;
> or close, in opposing lanes, at a hundred-and-thirty,
>
> trusting implicitly in simple self-interest, missing
> each other, time after time, only by fragments of seconds,
> as we move our lives, or dyings, another round toward
> what March may be like in maybe the year 2000.

Yes, the roads are dangerous, these lines acknowledge, but no one wants to die, and we can depend on each other's self-interest to keep us alive.

This vision of interdependence is common in Western culture. In sociological terms, it is often called Western individualism; in economic terms, the free-market economy. In America this view has prevailed for at least two hundred years, though of late its economic version has not been faring so well. But there is another vision of interdependence, which the Vietnamese Zen master Thich Nhat Hanh describes in this way:

In our ordinary discriminatory world, we see a teapot as a single, independent object. But when we look deeply enough into the teapot, we will see that it contains many phenomena—earth, water, fire, air, space, and time—and we will realize that in fact the entire universe has come together to make this teapot. That is the interdependent nature of the teapot. A flower is made up of many non-flower elements, such as clouds, soil, and sunshine. Without clouds and earth, there could be no flower. This is interbeing. The one is the result of the all. What makes the all possible is the one.

In this vision of interdependence, everything depends on everything else. All are interconnected parts of the great, indivisible body of reality, in which energies are constantly being exchanged, and what we normally call "things" are being transformed, moment by moment. To describe that reality, Thich Nhat Hanh has coined the word "interbeing."

In Japanese Zen, the reality of "interbeing" is epitomized by the Japanese word "mu," which literally means "no" but in Zen usage has no extractable content. Rather, it is a way of pointing toward things as they are at any given moment— impermanent, void of intrinsic selves, and utterly dependent upon each other. In contrast to "me," "mu" evokes a fundamental mutuality and engenders a spirit of compassion. Were I to see it on a license plate, I would feel safer on the road.

July 2, 2009

111

Without Ideals or Violence

*I*f you have looked closely at advertising copy, you may have noticed how often the word *perfect* appears in printed ads, whether the product be an appliance, an item for the garden, or a vacation rental. For only $18.97 you can own Black and Decker's 2-Slice Toaster with Electronic Shade Control, which will provide you with "perfect toast and bagels every time." If you would like to spruce up your lawn, Patch Perfect Grass Seed will ensure "perfect even coverage every time." If travel is on your horizon, Summer House on Winter Bay, a rental property on Prince Edward Island, offers "the perfect choice for your golfing group, family reunion, or destination wedding." And if you would like to enhance your experience of Zen meditation, you can buy a Mountain Timer from Zen Mountain Monastery at a cost of $145.00, plus shipping and handling. Designed to free you from glancing at a clock, the Mountain Timer is the "perfect complement to the stillness of meditation."

As these examples suggest, the word *perfect* (together with *ideal,* its first cousin) has become a buzzword in the advertising business, if not a mantra. Presumably, the word has become prominent because it has proven to be effective. What does its prominence tell us about its targeted clientele, namely ourselves?

The most obvious answer is that advertising appeals to our desires, and we would like the objects of those desires to be perfect, or as close to perfect as possible. Why settle for burnt toast or mediocre bagels? Why put up with a spotty lawn or a less-than-perfect vacation spot? And why use a stick of incense (the traditional method for timing a sitting) when you can have the perfect complement of a Mountain Timer? Fueling our fantasies, the word *perfect* feeds and creates our appetites and longings.

At a more covert level, the word also sends the message that our present lives—and by extension, our present selves—are woefully imperfect. By buying the perfect toaster we will help to remedy that remediable situation. By becoming smart, informed consumers, we will fill the vacancies in our daily round. By investing in a perfect future, we will relieve our present suffering.

As can be seen in the ad for the Mountain Timer, American Zen has not been impervious to Western consumer culture. On the contrary, meditation has often been sold as a form of stress reduction or promoted as a mode of self-improvement. But the primary aim of Zen practice is not to reduce stress or to place new heads, as one of the teachings puts it, on top of our present ones. Rather, it is to cultivate a clear and stable awareness of what is going on, within and without, and to free ourselves from our negative conditioning. And if one persists in the practice, what one is likely to see, clearly and unequivocally, is the connection between our conditioned images of perfection and the suffering we inflict on others and ourselves.

"My love, she speaks like silence," Bob Dylan sang in 1965, "without ideals or violence." In the same song ("Love Minus Zero / No Limit"), he contrasted his lover's serene self-containment with the dissatisfaction of "bankers' nieces" who "seek perfection / expecting all the gifts that wise men bring." Over the past four decades, we have witnessed the horrific violence that misguided idealism can loose upon the world. And in the past year we have seen the economic ruin that unbridled greed can foster. Looking inward, can we also see how unexamined notions of perfection lead us to destroy our happiness, impose unrealistic expectations on ourselves and others, and devalue our present lives? Can we learn to live more wisely?

July 16, 2009

Travels

_F_ or many people, summer is the season for travel. And for those who practice a contemplative discipline, travel can be a catalyst for spiritual growth. The seventeenth-century poet Basho, master of haiku and author of _The Narrow Road to the Deep North,_ believed that "nothing is worth noting that is not seen with fresh eyes." His extensive travels freshened and enlarged his vision. Thomas Merton had similar experiences in Asia, as recorded in his _Asian Journal._

Yet for those whose primary discipline is Zen meditation, travel can also present a formidable challenge. Insofar as the practice of Zen requires us to sit still, and travel requires us to be on the move, Zen and travel appear to be at odds. How might the one support the other? How might the practice of Zen be integrated with the experience of travel?

To begin with, the practice of meditation can alleviate the anxiety of travel. One of my friends told me the story of being in an international airport on a day when many flights had been canceled. People were berating ticket agents, yelling into their cell phones, and experiencing general misery. Then, as it happened, the Vietnamese Zen master Thich Nhat Hanh arrived in his brown robes, accompanied by the monks and nuns of Plum Village. Silent, gentle, and slow-moving, their presence transformed their environment. People quieted down.

Not everyone, of course, can be so fortunate as to have a troupe of Zen monastics on hand to relieve the fear of travel. But meditative practice, as taught by Thich Nhat Hanh, can calm the fearful mind. As he explains in his book by that title, we can lessen our anxieties not by drugging them with Valium or Johnnie Walker but by honestly acknowledging them and bringing a kind attention to their presence. "Breathing in, I am aware of my anxiety. / Breathing out, I bring kind attention to my anxiety." Over time, this simple practice can help to diminish the anxiety of travel.

So can the practice of sitting still, even when surrounded by incessant movement. Meditation is often described as a way of "stopping" and "coming home." By sitting still and following our breathing, we return to the stability of immovable awareness. We restore our equanimity. To be sure, it can be awkward to stop when everyone else is moving or to sit perfectly still in a public place. But we can find ways to sit still without calling attention to ourselves. And more often than not, passers-by are too preoccupied with their own affairs to care whether we are moving or sitting still.

Beyond the maintenance of personal balance, Zen practice can also deepen the experience of travel. In an earlier column I described the exercise of asking "What is this?" and regarding the things of this world as if we were seeing them for the first time. When traveling, we really *are* seeing things for the first time—and quite possibly the last. By asking "What is this?" we become present for whatever we are seeing, be it a glacier in Alaska or a cathedral in Madrid. And the places we see, in turn, become present for us. Later on, we can learn their names and study their histories. But by asking "What is this?" we open ourselves to our immediate experience.

Eihei Dogen, founder of the Soto school of Zen, cautioned against unnecessary travel. "It is futile to travel," he advised, "to dusty countries, thus forsaking your own seat." But Dogen was hardly one to talk, being himself a traveler who sojourned in dusty China and brought the practice of Chan back to Japan. And for the resourceful practitioner, travel can become a form of "skillful means," complementary to sitting meditation and consistent with its purpose.

May your travels be safe and your flights on time.

July 23, 2009

Resting

"**D**uring our sitting meditation," writes Zen master Thich Nhat Hanh in "Resting in the River," "we can allow ourselves to rest like a pebble. We can allow ourselves to sink naturally without effort to the position of sitting, the position of resting. Resting is a very important practice; we have to learn the art of resting."

In *A Conservationist Manifesto*, his new collection of essays on environmental issues, Scott Russell Sanders offers an evocative variation on this theme. Drawing on both his personal experience and his extensive knowledge of the Judeo-Christian tradition, Sanders likens meditative practice to the observance of the Sabbath. In both, he notes, we rest from our labors. In both, we "grant rest to all those beings … whose labor serves us."

The word Sabbath, Sanders reminds us, comes from a Hebrew root meaning "to rest." And in an essay entitled "Wilderness as a Sabbath for the Land," he examines the nuances of the word, drawing on relevant passages from the books of Exodus, Deuteronomy, and Leviticus. According to those sources, the Sabbath is, as Sanders puts it, a time to "lay down our tools, cease our labors, and set aside our plans, so that we may enjoy the sweetness of *being* without *doing*." But it is also a time to reenact the liberation of the Hebrew people "for the benefit of everyone and everything under their control." For the Earth and the laborer alike, the Sabbath is a restorative, affording "medicine for soil and spirit, a healing balm."

Turning to the New Testament, Sanders recalls the stories of Jesus offending the Pharisees by healing on the Sabbath. As Sanders sees it, "Jesus interpreted the Sabbath as a day for the breaking of fetters," and "instead of dwelling on what was forbidden, he dwelt on what was required—the relief of suffering, the restoring of health." When he proclaimed that "the Sabbath was made for humankind, and not humankind for the Sabbath," he was "recalling the spirit of freedom and jubilee implicit in the gift of the Sabbath." For the Sabbath, in this interpretation, is not only a day of rest, in which we are restored to a state of wholeness. It is also a day "for deliverance ... from whatever entraps us."

In "Stillness," a closely related essay, Sanders directly links the keeping of the Sabbath with the practice of meditation. Recounting the experience of sitting peacefully in a hut in the woods, he describes his sense of intimacy with the natural world:

> I wish to bear in mind all the creatures that breathe, which is why I've chosen to make my retreat here within the embrace of meadow and woods. The panorama I see through the windows is hardly wilderness, and yet every blade of grass, every grasshopper, every sparrow and twig courses

with a wild energy. The same energy pours through me. Although my body grows calm from sitting still, I rock slightly with the slow pulse of my heart. My ears fill with the pulse of crickets and cicadas proclaiming their desires. My breath and the clouds ride the same wind.

As he reflects on this experience, Sanders is reminded of the Sabbath and the injunction that every fiftieth year, the earth be granted a "solemn rest." And he suggests that "whatever our religious views, we might do well to recover the idea of the Sabbath, not only because we could use a solemn day of rest once a week but also because Earth could use a respite from our demands."

To be sure, the practice of meditation is not only one of rest and healing. It is also one of dynamic inquiry. But by invoking the idea of the Sabbath, Sanders provides an illuminating paradigm for meditative practice. What begins in solitude conduces to an awareness of the earth's manifold inhabitants. What begins in rest conduces to liberation.

August 13, 2009

The Way It Is

*S*ince the death of Walter Cronkite in July, much has been written about the late anchorman's moral authority. According to a Roper poll taken in 1974, Walter Cronkite was "the most trusted man in America." When he gravely intoned his signature line, we believed him. However shocking or sad the reality just reported, that's the way it was. The CBS Evening News with Walter Cronkite had opened a window on things as they were.

Zen practice also aims to put the practitioner in touch with reality, as it is in this very moment. And every Zen center or monastery has, as it were, its own Walter Cronkite. Whether he or she is called Abbot, Sensei, Roshi, or simply "head teacher," the person in this position embodies the inherited wisdom and the venerable authority of the Zen tradition. If the person is a "lineage holder," which is to say, has received "Dharma transmission" from an earlier teacher, the weight of authority is even greater. It is, in most instances, unquestioned, and one of the core requirements of a prospective Zen student is to believe in the teacher. If a Zen student is unable to do that, the student is well-advised to find another teacher.

Yet if the structure of the traditional zendo is authoritarian, the practice itself is quite the opposite. It is radically egalitarian. From the start, Zen students are enjoined to rely on direct experience: to trust their senses, not the words of any teacher. Every morning, students in Rinzai Zen training chant the verses *"Atta dipa / Viharata / Atta sirana / Ananna sirana,"* which roughly translate as "You are the Light / Rely on yourself / Rely on nothing but yourself." This is followed by *"Dhamma dipa / Dhamma sirana / Ananna sirana,"* which translates as "Rely on the Dharma / Rely on nothing but the Dharma." Although the word Dharma has multiple meanings, in this context it is best understood as "reality," or "the laws of reality," most prominently those of impermanence and interdependence. It is left to us to perceive those laws— and to realize ourselves within our immediate surroundings. As one ancient Chinese master told his student, "I can't wear clothes for you. I can't eat for you... I can't carry your body around and live your life for you." We must do these things— and *know* we doing them—ourselves.

How, then, is the near-absolute authority of the Zen teacher to be reconciled with the imperative to trust direct experience and rely on ourselves? And to the extent that we embrace a particular Zen lineage, to what extent are we free to question its authority? To speak for ourselves?

For Toni Packer, who left the Rochester Zen Center to establish the Springwater Center for Meditative Inquiry, the resolution lay in dropping the liturgy, forms, and hierarchies of traditional Japanese Zen, leaving only the sitting, listening, and questioning. For traditionalists, however, the resolution

lies not in discarding hierarchical structures but in clearly defining the teacher's role. Often that role is likened to a mir-
ror, which reflects the present state of the student's mind and
heart.

In my own experience, the most helpful teachers have
been those who have urged their students to look honestly
into their lives, moment by moment, and to act in accordance
with what they see. Rather than answer abstract questions
with absolute authority, such teachers return their students,
time and again, to the concrete, reliable practice of zazen: to
a direct and continuous contact with reality, just as it is. Only
then can the student realize the richness and depth of present
experience. Only then can he or she say, with any real authority, "That's the way it is."

August 27, 2009

Taking Care

*I*f you have lived in America for the past two decades you have almost certainly been enjoined to *take care*. Among contemporary American expressions, that benign valediction ranks with *Have a nice day* in frequency of use, and it is often used in much the same way. What we are supposed to take care of is left unspecified, but that is beside the point. Take care of everything, the phrase might well be saying, until we meet again.

Zen teachings also admonish us to take care. In her book *Mindfully Green*, the environmentalist Stephanie Kaza provides a vivid example:

> *In Zen kitchens, students are trained in what is called "knife practice," that is, how to take care of knives properly. First, this means noticing the properties of the knife while you are using it—its weight, its sharp edge, the way it feels in the hand, how it cuts. Then, when you're done with the knife, it means washing and drying it immediately and putting it back in the chopping block to keep the*

*knife safe. Doing this practice faithfully changes your rela-
tionship with knives. You are practicing caretaking as an
investment in the well-being of things. This is the opposite
of consuming things until they are gone.*

As here described, "knife practice" exemplifies conservation
and ecological awareness. Taking care of our kitchen knives,
we also take care of the planet Earth.

Knife practice is but one instance of *samu*, or work practice, which is as integral to Zen as sitting meditation. In Zen
centers and monasteries, residents and guests alike devote at
least an hour a day to caretaking: to scrubbing steps, cleaning
bathrooms, chopping vegetables, and other mundane chores.
As a practical matter, these daily labors keep the zendo clean
and running smoothly. Beyond that, they train Zen students
to "lower the mast of the ego," respect the humblest pot or
pail, and concentrate on one thing at a time. Performed in
silence and with full awareness, work practice prompts the
practitioner to examine conventional notions of low and
high, menial and exalted labor. And as an embodiment of an
ethic, it extends beyond the zendo into domestic life, where
the same principle may be applied to the care of a house or
garden, bicycle or car.

The ethical principle of "taking care" also extends beyond the care of material objects. Broadly interpreted, it
includes the care of one's body, mind, and heart, moment
by moment, through the practice of meditation. Zen master
Thich Nhat Hanh puts it this way:

*To meditate means to go home to yourself. Then you know
how to take care of the things that are happening inside
you, and you know how to take care of the things that*

125

are happening around you. All meditation exercises are aimed at bringing you back to your true home, to yourself. Without restoring your peace and calm and helping the world restore peace and calm, you cannot go very far in the practice.

In keeping with this admonition, Thich Nhat Hanh directs us to bring awareness to the parts of our bodies, moving systematically from the eyes to the lungs to the heart, and so on. In another exercise, we bring awareness to our sensations, noting whether they are pleasant, unpleasant, or neutral. And in another, we attend to our states of mind, including those of anxiety and anger. If we are experiencing the latter, we are urged to take care of it, as a parent might care for a crying child. Rather than vent or suppress our anger, we bring a gentle attention to its presence. By so doing, we allow its energies to disperse or to change into something more constructive.

The wisdom of Zen is not confined to arcane koans or ancient Chinese stories or the cryptic sayings of the masters. It also resides in everyday life—or, in this case, in the commonest of American expressions. So may I suggest that when you hear that expression, you regard it not as an empty cliché but as wise and timely advice. Let it remind you to take care.

September 10, 2009

Awareness and Conjecture

*D*uring my thirty-eight years as a teacher of literature and writing, I read and corrected thousands of papers, essays, poems, and stories. Understandably, most of those words have long been forgotten. Now and then, however, a phrase coined by a student will arise out of memory, for reasons I can seldom explain.

That happened recently, as I recalled a phrase from a student's poem. *Nor sullied by conjecture*, is what she wrote, some thirty years ago. And though I can't recall the specific context, I find myself dwelling on the phrase itself, partly because its two main words, uncommon at the time, have grown increasingly rare, and partly because the phrase has a bearing on the practice of Zen.

Derived from the same root as "soil," the word sully means "to pollute, defile, stain, or tarnish." Shakespeare uses the word often, as in *A Winter's Tale* , where Leontes abhors an act that would "Sully the purity and whiteness of [his] sheets," or in Sonnet 15, where the forces of Time and Decay threaten to change his youthful subject's "day of youth to sullied night." In his first soliloquy, Hamlet expresses the wish that his "too too solid flesh might melt, / Thaw, and resolve itself into a dew." Scholars are still uncertain whether Shakespeare wrote "solid" or "sullied." The former is more consistent with the images of melting and thawing, but the latter is the more evocative.

Conjecture is also an arresting word. If it's used at all nowadays, its context is usually formal or academic. A conjecture is an educated guess. Or a not-so-educated guess. Or, as defined by the *American Heritage Dictionary,* an "inference based on inconclusive or incomplete evidence." The root of the word is the Latin *jacere,* which means "to throw." Combined with the prefix *con,* which here means "together," the word's origins evoke an image of something hastily constructed—something *thrown together,* often with more ingenuity than concrete evidence. For examples, we need only watch cable news, particularly in the months before an election, or when a celebrity has been charged with a crime, or when someone has gone missing.

Such are the meanings of *sully* and *conjecture,* taken singly. But what might their combination mean, as the phrase relates to Zen meditation? What, exactly, might be sullied by conjecture, and by whom?

Imagine, if you will, that just as you are falling asleep, the village siren sounds its alarm. You wake, a little groggy. Is someone's house on fire? Has someone been in a serious accident? Or has someone burned a bag of popcorn in a microwave and set off a smoke alarm?

Those are conjectures, prompted by a sound. What is actual is the sound itself—its spiraling crescendo, its long sustained note, its sinking into silence. The rest is fabrication, the work of the ever-thinking mind. And what is being sullied, as it were, is pure awareness, in this instance awareness of a sound. Lost in conjecture, we may scarcely hear that sound—or be fully aware of the thoughts and feelings it has just aroused.

To cultivate pure awareness is a primary aim of Zen meditation. Hindering that awareness are the ego's ceaseless machinations, which include not only conjecture but also expectation, speculation, fantasizing, and escape into abstract thought. All of these mental activities, habitual and sometimes obsessive, distract us from seeing and hearing what is going on, within and around us. Yet with practice it is possible to live in full awareness much of the time, including a real-time awareness of the mind's insididous deceptions. And though the odds are against it, it is possible to cultivate the concomitant of that awareness: a clear and balanced mind, unhindered by fear and unsullied by conjecture.

September 24, 2009

A Mighty Wave

One afternoon in August I waded into the ocean at Dewey Beach, Delaware. Under the hot sun, the waist-high breakers crashed against me. To steady myself, I adopted a T'ai Chi stance, keeping my center of gravity low. Wading just behind me was my wife, Robin, who is sometimes quite excitable.

"Oh, my God!" Robin exclaimed.

Thinking that she had seen something unusual on the beach—a three-legged dog, perhaps—I looked over my shoulder. The next thing I knew, I was lying flat on my back in the water, looking up at the blue sky. A mighty wave had struck me down.

However startling, my experience was not uncommon. Nor is it unusual, in these times, for people who thought they were on a steady footing to be knocked flat by an unexpected force, whether the mighty wave take the form of a lost job, a foreclosed home, or a frightening diagnosis. When such things happen, of what use is the practice of Zen?

If you have tried meditation and found it foreign or difficult or boring, your answer might well be "very little." But as
a longtime practitioner, I would suggest three ways in which
Zen and other forms of meditation can help us cope with
adversity.

First and most obvious, meditation steadies the mind.
That is particularly true of the concentrative forms of meditation, which include concentration on the breath, an image,
or a mantra. Even a few minutes of concentrative meditation
can leave the practitioner feeling calmer, steadier, and more
in control. The effect may be temporary, but over time this
form of meditation, diligently practiced, engenders stability
of mind. In Zen teachings, meditative stability is likened to
that of a mountain, which remains immovable in all kinds of
weather.

Beyond the cultivation of stability, meditative practice
tends to promote a realistic outlook. Having trained ourselves, day after day, in seeing the impermanence of all conditioned things, we are not so surprised when something that
appeared to be permanent proves otherwise. Having learned
to be present without expectations, we are better prepared
for the unexpected. And having cultivated an openness to all
experience, pleasant and painful, we can deal more realisti-
cally with the latter when it comes our way. So it was with
Darlene Cohen, the author of several books on living with
chronic pain, who had practiced Zen for six years before she
was diagnosed with crippling rheumatoid arthritis. "I turned
toward the disease," she explains, "and its impact on my
body / mind as a mindfulness practice."

In keeping with the realism that daily practice encour-
ages, Zen meditation can also help us see that what occurs

is often not so personal as it first appears. In a well-known Zen story, a man is rowing his boat on a lake when a fog sets in. He continues to row, maintaining his course as best he can. Then, suddenly and unexpectedly, another vessel crashes into his. Furious, he curses. "You fool!" he yells into the fog. "Look what you've done to my new boat!" But moments later, he discovers that the other boat is empty. What happened simply happened.

The point of that story is not that we have no responsibility for the damage we cause or incur. We do. But what the story illustrates—and what meditative practice teaches—is that much of our suffering is self-inflicted. We cannot always control what happens to us, but through continuing practice we can recognize the role that egoistic delusion plays in our responses. It is enough to have one's brand-new boat damaged by another. To assume, reflexively, that the circumstances were personal only adds to one's distress.

In my own case, a mighty wave struck me down, not because Providence, Fate, or some other force had singled me out, but because I was in a certain place at a certain time, and I wasn't paying attention. As it happened, I was listening to my wife, which under most other circumstances would have been a good thing to do.

October 8, 2009

Closing Doors

*T*here are many ways to close a door. It can be done angrily or in haste. It can be done with infinite care. When Thich Nhat Hanh, then a young Vietnamese monk, visited the Trappist monk Thomas Merton at the Abbey of Gethsemani in Kentucky in 1966, Merton observed how his guest opened and closed the door. From that action alone, Merton later remarked, he could tell that Thich Nhat Hanh was "an authentic monk."

Presumably, Thich Nhat Hanh closed the door quietly and with full attention, as his monastic training had taught him to do. In his book *Zen Keys*, he explains the purpose of that training:

The master can see if the student is or is not "awake." If, for example, a student shuts the door noisily or carelessly, he is demonstrating a lack of mindfulness. Closing the door gently is not in itself a virtuous act, but awareness of the fact that you are closing the door is an expression of real practice. In this case, the master simply reminds the student to close the door gently, to be mindful. The master does this not only to respect the quiet of the monastery, but to point out to the student that he was not practicing mindfulness, that his actions were not majestic or subtle.

Although he is articulating a general principle, Thich Nhat Hanh is also recalling a personal experience. As a sixteen-year-old novice, he closed a door with less than full attention, and his teacher called him back for a second try. That experience was, in his words, his "first lesson in the practice of mindfulness."

In Zen practice the closing of a door is only one of some ninety thousand "subtle gestures," each an expression of mindfulness. Symbolically, however, the opening or closing of a door has special importance, insofar as it signifies a moment of transition. In his poem "Men at Forty" the American poet Donald Justice employs that traditional symbol, as he observes that "Men at forty / Learn to close softly / The doors to rooms / They will not be coming back to." As they stand "At rest on a stair landing," these newly middle-aged men "feel it moving / Beneath them now like the deck of a ship, / Though the swell is gentle."

In her book *Making Friends with Death*, Judith Lief employs the same symbol to describe the transitions in our lives:

Transitions are like doorways. When we open a door, we think we know what we will find on the other side, but we can never be sure. We do not know with certainty whether we will find a friend or an enemy, an obstacle or an opportunity. Without actually opening the door and walking through, we have no way of knowing. When we face such a door, we feel uncertain, vulnerable, exposed. Our usual

strategies do not hold. We are in no-man's-land. Transi-
tions make us uncomfortable, and they are often accom-
panied by some degree of pain, but at the same time, they
open us to new possibilities.

Acknowledging that each moment of experience is a transition, "bounded by its own birth and death," Lief reminds us that transitions often engender fear. Like Justice's forty-year-olds on their moving decks, we feel uncertain and insecure. As a counter-measure, Lief urges us to pay close attention to all the transitions in our lives, however small, and to abide, if we can, in uncertainty, rather than retreat to what we know. By so doing, we "begin to loosen our habitual fear of the unknown and undefined."

For many of us, that noble goal is not so easily attained. It is one thing to learn, as Thich Nhat Hanh did, how to close a door with full attention. It is another to learn how to witness and accept transitions, whether they be from youth to middle age, working life to retirement, robust health to chronic illness, a stable marriage to sudden widowhood. But, in truth, the two kinds of learning are of a piece, and the one is training for the other. By learning to be mindful of the "ninety thousand subtle gestures," we cultivate an ability to cope with the not-so-subtle changes that befall us. By learning to close an actual door with full awareness, we strengthen our capacity to pass, with grace and affirmation, through the wider doorways that lie ahead.

October 22, 2009

135

Chazen Ichimi

*F*or at least eight centuries the practice of Zen has
been closely linked to the consumption of green
tea. In 1191 the Zen monk Eisai returned to Kyoto
from his studies in China, bringing a bag of tea seeds, which
he planted in the temple garden. In 1211 he wrote *Kissa Yojoki*
(*The Book of Tea*), Japan's first tea book, extolling the health-
fulness of green tea. Ever since, Zen practitioners have used
green tea to nurture their bodies, soothe their minds, and keep
themselves awake during their long hours of sitting. *"Chazen
ichimi,"* declared the sixteenth-century tea master Sen Sotan:
"Zen and the taste of tea are one and the same."

Over the past two decades, health-conscious Americans
have also brought green tea into their daily lives, but where
taste is concerned, the reviews have been decidedly mixed.
"Would you drink green tea," a skeptical friend once asked,
"if you didn't know it was good for you?" And another, whose
taste in beverages runs to single-malt Scotch and a good Mer-
lot, reported that he tried green tea and it tasted like paste-
board. If that is the taste of Zen, so much the worse for Zen.

If you too have tried green tea and found it not to your liking, that may be the end of the matter. However, if you already drink green tea but would like to enjoy it more, you can do so by making a small investment in equipment and by following a few time-honored instructions. With patience, care, and a little practice, you might find yourself enjoying a delicious, authentic cup of Japanese green tea.

First of all, you will need fresh tea. What is available in the supermarket or even in specialty tea shops is often anything but fresh. It may have been languishing in a tea bag or bin for a very long time. I order tea directly from Hibiki-an (*www.hibiki-an-com*), a family-owned firm in Kyoto, and it arrives in a few days, sealed in a foil-lined bag. When I open the bag, the aroma of the unbrewed tea is itself enticing.

Second, you will need a *kyusu*, an earthenware teapot designed expressly for brewing green tea. For the price of a coffeemaker you can buy a kyusu online, and it's well worth the expense. The distinguishing features of the kyusu include its hollow side handle and its interior mesh filter, which covers the opening of the spout. In contrast to the familiar infuser, the latter feature allows the tea leaves to open and to float freely in the water, releasing their flavor.

Third, you will need the softest, purest water you can find. Hibiki-an recommends Evian, Rocky Mountain, and other bottled waters. Here in Western New York, I use Chemung Spring Water, and it has proved equal to the task.

Fourth, you will need to pay attention to the temperature and the brewing time. On most mornings I drink a refreshing Sencha tea, which is brewed at 176 degrees Fahrenheit for sixty to eighty seconds. Other teas require other temperatures and brewing times. At first, you will need to use a thermometer and to watch the time very carefully. Later on, you can dispense with the thermometer, and you can adjust the prescribed time to suit your taste.

To prepare two cups of Sencha tea, you will need a kyusu and three small teacups. To brew the tea, please follow these instructions:

—Boil the water, let it cool for a minute, and pour it into the kyusu. When the water has cooled for another minute, pour it into two of the three cups. Drain any remaining water from the kyusu.

—Next, pour the water back and forth among the three cups. This process heats the cups and further cools the water. It also allows the water to oxygenate, which improves the flavor of the tea.

—Check the temperature. When it is around 176 degrees, add a tablespoon of loose Sencha tea to the heated kyusu and pour in just enough water to cover the leaves. Replace the lid, and wait for twenty seconds, letting the leaves absorb the water. Then add the rest of the water, and brew for a minute or slightly longer.

—Now pour the tea alternately into two of the cups, and offer one to your guest. Lifting your own cup with both hands, take time to inhale the aroma of the tea. Contemplate its provenance, its impermanence, and its beneficial influence on your mind and body. Then drink it slowly, with full attention, and enjoy the taste of Zen.

November 5, 2009

The Tempo of Meditation

*P*atience, we are told, is a virtue. As a child growing up in eastern Iowa, I heard that bromide more than once. However, as an adolescent I learned about patience not from listening to Methodist sermons or elders' proverbs but by spending time with an exceptionally patient man.

His name was Sven Jorgensen, and he was the co-owner of Eble and Jorgensen Office Supply, where I worked after school, on weekends, and in the summers. Unlike Fred Eble, a former Navy Seabee and a tense, frenetic striver, Sven exuded steadiness and calm. Wiry, high-strung Fred dealt with the public and could often be found in the front of the store, filling out orders or talking on the phone. Thick-set, sedentary Sven worked quietly at his table in the back room, cleaning and repairing typewriters. Nearby was a photo of Sven and his dog Walt in a flat-bottomed fishing boat. Like his owner, Walt looked stable and relaxed.

To everyone in town, Sven Jorgensen was known as Speed. Speed Jorgensen. He acquired that name at the age of fourteen, when he barreled down a steep hill on his bike, rode into a pile of frozen leaves, and flew over the handlebars. He hadn't realized that the leaves were frozen. Ever after, all physical evidence to the contrary, Sven would be known as Speed. It was a lifelong joke, played by the world on a slow-moving Swede.

At Eble and Jorgensen's I sometimes waited on customers, made deliveries, or stocked shelves, but much of the time I worked in the back room, where dirty or broken typewriters waited to be restored. With his big Swedish hands Speed would carry them, one by one, to his table, where he put them in a deep tray half-filled with solvent. There he would clean their typebars with a solvent-soaked toothbrush, adjust their springs, replace broken or tarnished keys. When he was finished, even the most abused machine would function smoothly and look as good as new.

Much of the time, Speed worked silently, as did I, but sometimes we chatted as we worked. Or rather, I talked and Speed listened, offering advice when advice was sorely needed. Once, when I had manged to deliver rubber cement rather than duplicating fluid to an office, nearly precipitating a crisis, Speed sharply admonished me to be more attentive. On another occasion, when I was enumerating my father's faults, Speed remarked, without looking up, that my father was a very nice man. And once, when I repeated a mean-spirited joke I'd heard at school, he told me in so many words that my joke was not very funny. I would not repeat it again.

In his unchosen role as friend and mentor, Speed taught partly by precept but mostly by example. What he exemplified was not only patience but also the virtue of slowing down, even when typewriters needed to be cleaned or supplies delivered. Working slowly but productively at his table, or pausing in his work to offer kind advice, he provided vivid proof that life could be lived at a slower pace, allowing time to look more deeply and act more wisely.

The pace at which Sven Jorgensen lived and worked is also the pace of meditation. "Do you have the patience to wait," asks Lao-Tzu in the *Tao Te Ching*, "till your mud settles and the water is clear? / Can you remain unmoving / till the right action arises by itself?" And in his book *Meditation as Contemplative Inquiry*, the physicist Arthur Zajonc observes that "hurrying is antithetical to the required tempo of meditation." Elaborating that point, he notes that "the tempo of meditation is the same as that of artistic attention; it is the rhythm of poetry. Speed hides all subtlety; and reality is subtle."

Which of us isn't in a hurry? Although my son once referred to me as his slow-moving dad, I too can get in a rush, lose all patience, and miss the subtleties of experience. If I need a retardant, I can find it in the image of Lao-Tzu, writing immortal poetry in his mountain retreat. Or, closer to home, I can call back the memory of Speed Jorgensen at his table, patiently scrubbing an ink-filled "o," or winding a cloth ribbon on a spool, or calmly wiping a well-worn platen.

November 19, 2009

Weathered Wood

*I*n our culture, new is usually considered better. And where so-called home improvements are concerned, that is often the case, especially if the new item is a high-efficiency furnace or a forty-year roof or an energy-saving kitchen appliance. But sometimes the situation is more complex than that, the effect more problematic.

Recently we installed new vinyl windows in our home. In contrast to the fifty-year-old relics they replaced, the new windows bring a soft, expansive light into our darker rooms. Gone are the small panes and splintered mullions. Gone, too, are the uncaulked cracks and loose-fitting frames that let out heat. Our house feels tighter now, and our carbon footprint will almost certainly be smaller.

Yet with this welcome change has come an unexpected loss. Clean and efficient though they are, our new windows lack a quality that was palpably present in the decrepit pine windows they replaced. In American parlance that quality is sometimes called "character," and it is said to reside in such objects as weathered deck chairs, antique tools, and Willie

Nelson's battered guitar. Our rattling old windows, such as they were, had character; our new vinyl windows, whatever their environmental virtues, do not.

In Japanese culture, the quality I'm describing is known as *sabi*, and it has an integral connection to the practice of Zen. Often linked with *wabi*, which connotes simplicity and a life free of materialistic striving, *sabi* once meant "loneliness" or "solitude." In modern usage, it means the quality of being old, worn, and faded—and all the more beautiful for the wear and tear. The architect Tadao Ando defines the quality in this way:

> *Sabi by itself means "the bloom of time." It connotes natural progression—tarnish, hoariness, rust—the extinguished gloss of that which once sparkled. It's the understanding that beauty is fleeting ... Sabi things carry the burden of their years with dignity and grace: the chilly mottled surface of an oxidized silver bowl, the yielding gray of weathered wood, the elegant withering of a bereft autumn bough.*

Noting that sabi "transcends the Japanese," Ando finds it in "an old car left in a field to rust, as it transforms from an eyesore into a part of the landscape." This, he suggests, might be considered "America's contribution to the evolution of sabi."

Beyond the aspect of age, the word sabi also connotes imperfection. Rooted historically in the tea ceremony, the aesthetic of sabi developed in the sixteenth century as an indigenous reaction to the expensive teaware imported from China. In contrast to the brilliant colors and ostentatious perfection of Chinese wares and utensils, the tea masters Murata Shuko, Takeno Jo-o, and especially Sen no Rikyu (1522–1591) introduced such rough, imperfect objects as stoneware buckets and tea bowls produced by local craftsmen. In subsequent centuries, the aesthetic thus established extended to a general appreciation of imperfect objects, whether the object be a bamboo screen or a leaky vase. As the feudal baron Lord Fumai (1751–1819), himself the owner of a leaky vase, explained, "The *furyu* [*sabi*] of this bamboo vase consists in the very fact of this leakage."

Yet if the objects that embody *sabi* are imperfect, it is not because they were poorly made. Nor is their imperfection a sign of neglect. On the contrary, as Tadao Ando remarks, "*wabi-sabi* is never messy or slovenly," and an unmade bed or a room cluttered with junk is not an expression of *sabi*. Objects that possess *sabi* do so because they are visibly in the process of breaking down and reverting to the state of nature. Their imperfection is a mark of their impermanence. To contemplate sabi is to be reminded of the emptiness from which all things come and to which they will return. It is also to be reminded of the dynamic web of life, in which energies are constantly being exchanged, and new forms are coming into being.

The aesthetic of sabi and the practice of Zen are branches of a single cultural tree, and they have much in common. In both, a heightened awareness of impermanence draws us closer to the evanescent beauty of the present moment. In both, the pathos of things going in and out of existence mingles with a sense of infinite possibility. And in both, the realization that all things are transitory prompts us to value and care for our lives.

December 3, 2009

Silence and Intimacy

*I*f you are near-sighted, as I am, you may have found that you can sometimes see nearby objects more clearly by taking off your glasses. Or, to put it another way, in the absence of your glasses, the inherent closeness of those objects becomes more apparent. What was supposed to enhance your vision was actually imposing a veil between yourself and the coffee cup in front of you.

One of the aims of Zen practice is to recognize such veils and, if possible, to remove them. According to Zen teachings, direct experience of the world—or what the Zen-trained teacher Toni Packer calls "fresh seeing"—is the one reliable basis for knowledge, understanding, and whatever wisdom we might acquire. Books and teachers may guide us, confirm what we have seen, or place our perceptions in an enabling context. But we must see things for ourselves. In Zen practice we cultivate direct seeing and a sense of intimacy, both with ourselves and with the world around us. Whatever stands in the way is to be set aside, or subjected to scrutiny, or cut asunder.

Of the conditions conducive to direct seeing, none is more important than the silence of meditation. "Only when I am quiet for a long time / and do not speak," writes the poet Jane Hirshfield, "do the objects of my life draw near." Elaborating her theme, she imagines that the proximate objects in her life, among them scissors and spoons and a blue mug, are deliberately keeping their distance from her. Even her towels, "for all their intimate knowledge," are hesitant to come close. They are kept away by speech and thought, which separate self and other, the ego-centered mind and the things of this world. Only in those rare, egoless moments when she glimpses "for even an instant the actual instant" do the objects of her life draw near. At such moments, she fancifully suggests, each object emits a "sigh of happiness," knowing that she has joined "their circle of simple, passionate thusness," void of habitual, me-centered thought and the separation it imposes.

Such intimacy is indeed a source of happiness. Conversely, a sense of separation can engender a deep and chronic suffering. In her essay "Touching Fear" Toni Packer addresses that reality:

> "I'm never free of fear," some people say, implying that there should be a state of mind and body that is free of fear. How can we possibly be free from fear when we live in the conditioned mode of the me-story most of the time? We're deeply programmed to believe in this separate me by inaccurate language and by growing up in a world of other mes, all of whom think of and experience themselves as separate entities. ... With separation inevitably goes fear and pain.

Elsewhere, Packer quotes a questioner who asked, "Why does this *me*-ness, this self-centered feeling, arise when we realize that it causes such a painful sense of separation? How did it ever start in the first place?" Packer admits that she doesn't know, but she also suggests that "all of us can watch *me*-ness as it is arising from moment to moment. We can find out about it if we are really deeply interested and curious."

Perhaps we can. And perhaps over time we can also discover ways to release ourselves from the me-centered tyranny of dualistic thinking, which places images and concepts between ourselves and the objects in our lives. By sitting still and not speaking, if only for the space of an hour, we can permit those objects to draw near, and we can rejoin what the poet Mary Oliver has called the "family of things." By taking off our conceptual glasses, we can see the world afresh, and see our place within it.

December 17, 2009

A Sense of Arrival

I f you enjoy listening to the classical guitar, you may be familiar with the *Prelude* from J.S. Bach's *Prelude, Fugue and Allegro* (BMV 998), one of the most beautiful pieces in the standard repertoire. Composed for lute or harpsichord in the so-called "broken style" (*style brisé*) of the French Baroque, the *Prelude* consists largely of arpeggiated chords. Played evenly and deliberately, the successive notes create an impression of wholeness, as though the chords' original order had been restored.

Twenty-five years ago, I performed the *Prelude* in a master class at an international guitar festival in Toronto. The class was conducted by David Russell, then a rising star and now a concert artist of the highest distinction. Seated before me were some fifty guitarists and guitar teachers from around the world. To perform in such a setting was both exhilarating and daunting, not least because my audience had intimate knowledge of the piece I was playing. Interpretive felicities would not go unnoticed, but neither would mistakes.

Despite the stressful circumstances, I turned in a creditable performance. When I had finished, and the polite applause had died down, David Russell offered his critique.

To begin with, my tone had been inconsistent. I needed to work on that. Moreover, I had played the piece rather metrically, almost metronomically. I could allow myself and the music greater freedom. And most important, I had come down too hard at the ends of phrases. To avoid that unfortunate tendency, I might regard the last notes of phrases not as points of emphasis but as points of destination. "Think of them as *arrivals*," David suggested.

Given the character of the *Prelude,* David Russell's suggestion, however astute, was difficult to put into practice. Composed in 12/8 meter, the *Prelude* is marked by unceasing forward movement. With the exception of one long pause near the end, the score contains no moments of repose, no half notes, whole notes, or fermatas. If there are to be points of rest—points of arrival—the performer must consciously put them in. Or rather, the performer must be sensitive to natural, if reclusive, moments of repose.

In twenty-five years of playing the *Prelude,* I have never forgotten the principle articulated by David Russell. And over the years, I have seen how that principle may be applied in situations well beyond the bounds of musical interpretation, namely the practice of meditation and the conduct of everyday life.

With respect to meditation, Zen master Thich Nhat Hanh recommends that as we sit in stillness, we silently recite the verses, "I have arrived // I am home / In the here / And in the now," letting these phrases accompany our inhalations and exhalations. More simply, we can inwardly recite the

149

words "Arrive / home" and "Here / now" while breathing in and out. In that way, we counter the pressure, so prevalent in our culture, to be always on the move, always *en route* to somewhere else.

This practice is both pleasant and nourishing, and over time it can become an integral part of the daily round. Even the most hectic day contains moments of potential repose, in which we can cultivate a sense of arrival. And as with musical performance, we can honor those points of rest without losing our general momentum. By doing so, we may discover a hidden but inherent order, a rhythm akin to natural breathing. And we may also discover that even under the most anxious circumstances, it is possible to stop and collect ourselves before making our next move. Indeed, it is essential to do so, lest the life we've been given become little more than a shapeless, graceless succession of sixteenth-notes, played without meaning at breakneck speed.

January 7, 2010

Dropping into Awareness

*A*s I pick up my teacup on this cold winter morning, I'm remembering the story of the Zen student who asked Shunryu Suzuki, author of *Zen Mind, Beginner's Mind,* why the Japanese make their teacups so thin. Being so delicate, the cups are easily broken.

"It's not that they're too delicate," Suzuki Roshi replied, "but that you don't know how to handle them. You must adjust yourself to the environment, and not vice versa."

Suzuki's Roshi's point is well taken. We must adjust to our surroundings. However, if you are living in Western New York in the month of January, you may be feeling a little resistance to Suzuki's wisdom. It is not so difficult to adjust to one's environment when, as now, a lean female cardinal is coming and going from our feeder, her orange beak and tan feathers catching the early-morning light. But it is not so easy when your driveway is filled with snow, the sidewalks are icy, and you're already sick of scarves and parkas. Here in Alfred, New York, we know how to handle such conditions, but that doesn't mean we like them.

151

Yet the significance of the student's question and Suzuki's response transcends the question of adjustment. What the story vividly illustrates is the way in which preconceptions—in this instance, that teacups should be sturdy and equipped with handles—influence and often govern our perceptions. And it also exemplifies the resistance that many of us bring to the unknown, whether the new or foreign object be a Japanese teacup or an all-electric car.

For a more immediate example, please pause and consider any preconceptions that you might have brought to the reading of this column. Perhaps you expected something other than what you've encountered—a discussion of meditative methods, for instance, or an explanation of *satori*. Or, conversely, perhaps what you have so far read accords with your expectations, and you are more or less satisfied. In the first instance, you might choose to read something else; in the second, you might choose to read on.

There is, however, another option, which is to examine your expectations and your present response in the light of awareness. Looking closely into both, you can discern your assumptions, your fixed ideas, and the judgments they've engendered. And you can become aware of those mental processes, even as they are arising, continuing, and passing away.

In *The Four Foundations of Mindfulness,* a core text for Zen students, awareness of this kind is called "mindfulness of the mind in the mind." That somewhat cumbersome phrase refers to awareness of mental phenomena in the very moment when they are occurring. Such awareness is not the same as discursive thinking. Rather, it is a kind of effortless seeing, its object in this case being the thoughts that cross our minds. In contrast to fear, worry, and resistance, open awareness liberates the mind, both by illuminating our mental processes and by revealing the empty, or ephemeral, nature of mental events.

Such awareness cannot be awakened by an act of will. There is no switch to turn it on. However, it can be cultivated through the practices of sitting and walking meditation. And when it occurs, it can be felt in the mind as a spacious receptivity and in the body as a subtle shift of orientation—a shift from the confines of the head to the expansiveness of the *hara*, the body's center of gravity, situated in the lower abdomen. Viewed from the standpoint of the hara, even the most destructive thought loses much of its power.

Shinge Roko Sherry Chayat Roshi, Abbot of the Zen Center of Syracuse, has likened this felt shift from thinking to awareness to an expectant mother's experience of her baby "dropping" into the pelvis shortly before birth. In this instance, however, the baby is the mind itself, as it settles into awareness, fully cognizant of whatever is occurring. In that silent, open space, habitual thoughts and self-protective judgments can be recognized for what they are and nothing more. And even a traditional Japanese teacup, however breakable or difficult to handle, can be appreciated as something useful, beautiful, and new.

January 21, 2010

Looking Deeply

*A*ccording to the fifth-century Indian sage Bodhidharma, one of the founders of the Zen tradition, Zen is a mode of inquiry "not dependent on words and letters." It is a practice of direct seeing, based on direct experience. Language in general and conceptual language in particular can come between our minds and the realities of this world. We can mistake the word moon for the moon itself.

Yet, as Zen master Thich Nhat Hanh, author of more than sixty books, affirms, "Writing is a practice of looking deeply." Through the act of writing, as through the practice of meditation, we can become intimate with our lives. We can stop and look deeply into what is occurring, and as the poet Eavan Boland once put it, we can fully "experience our experience." In these ways, as in many others, the parallel practices of meditative inquiry and meditative writing share a common purpose. And in the works of the greatest contemplative writers—Thomas Merton, Rainer Maria Rilke, Elizabeth Bishop, Matsuo Basho, to name a few—the two practices are so closely allied as to be one and the same.

That is certainly true of the Irish Nobel laureate Seamus Heaney (b. 1939), whose poems and essays bear the marks of a meditative temperament. And in his poem "Personal Helicon," he offers an illuminating metaphor for the process of "looking deeply," even as his poem enacts that process.

The title of Heaney's poem alludes to Mount Helicon, the sanctuary of the Muses in Greek mythology. By association, it also alludes to the Hippocrene spring, the legendary source of poetic inspiration, which was situated on Mount Helicon. Yet at first glance the poem appears to be a fond sketch of childhood, set in rural County Derry and centering on the poet's early fascination with wells. "They could not keep me from wells," Heaney declares in his opening stanza. "I loved the dark drop, the trapped sky, the smells / Of waterweed, fungus and dank moss." In subsequent stanzas, he recalls particular wells in the Northern Irish countryside, including one "so deep you saw no reflection in it," and a shallow well in a ditch, which "fructified like any aquarium."

In his closing stanzas, however, Heaney turns from fond reminiscence to mature reflection on his life's work:

Others had echoes, gave back your own call
With a clean new music in it. And one
Was scaresome, for there, out of ferns and tall
Foxgloves, a rat slapped across my reflection.

Now, to pry into roots, to finger slime,
To stare, big-eyed Narcissus, into some spring
Is beneath all adult dignity. I rhyme
To see myself, to set the darkness echoing.

In the first of these stanzas, Heaney acknowledges both the childhood pleasure of hearing echoes in a well and the not-so-pleasant experience of seeing a rat in the water. Understood figuratively, the image of the rat suggests foul and frightening aspects of the self and the world, revealed by the process of looking deeply. And in the closing stanza, he likens that process to the act of writing, which allows him both to see himself and to evoke what he has elsewhere called "the mysterious otherness of the world." Like the child's voice echoing in a well, the mature poet's rhymes conjure the dark unknown. They create a state of mind known to literary analysts as "negative capability" and to Zen practitioners as "Don't-know mind" or the mind of "not-knowing." Abiding with confidence and courage in that state, the poet and meditative practitioner are open to infinite possibilities.

Not everyone can write a poem with the depth and precision of "Personal Helicon." But anyone with pen and paper can enlist the act of writing as a tool of meditative inquiry. As the American poet William Stafford once remarked, writing is "one of the great free human activities," which anyone can pursue, whether as a literary vocation or as a vehicle for "looking deeply." Please try it for yourself.

February 4, 2010

A Fundamental Perplexity

Since its arrival in the West, the practice of Zen has taken a rich variety of forms, ranging from the most traditional to the most iconoclastic. At one end of the spectrum there is formal Zen, with its incense, bows, and chants. At the other, there is "bare-bones" Zen, void of liturgy, hierarchy, or lineage.

Yet for all their differences, the varieties of Western Zen share a common practice, namely that of radical questioning. As Roshi Philip Kapleau, author of *The Three Pillars of Zen*, once put it, "the ultimate aim of Zen training is full awakening," and "to awaken, what is most essential is a questioning mind growing out of a fundamental perplexity, or 'ball of doubt'." That view is echoed by Zoketsu Norman Fischer, a contemporary Soto Zen priest, who defines the "core" of Zen as the "active, powerful, fundamental, relentless, deep and uniquely human act of questioning." Hearing these definitive statements, we might ask what "questioning," as practiced in Zen, is and is not, and how it might be enlisted in everyday life.

To begin with, Zen inquiry is not the questioning born of fear. Any thoughtful person who has gone through a divorce, the foreclosure of a home, or the loss of a job knows the experience of questioning what to do next, whom to blame, and how to survive a traumatic loss. Such questioning is necessary and sometimes productive, but it is not the questioning of Zen.

Second, Zen questioning is not the same as rigorous philosophical inquiry. To be sure, Zen teachings engage metaphysical issues, most prominently the "Great Matter of life and death." And insofar as they emphasize personal responsibility and freedom of choice, Zen teachings share common ground with existentialist thought. But unlike professional philosophy, Zen eschews definitions, abstract categories, and other components of systematic inquiry. Its way is more immediate, intuitive, personal, and concrete.

And third, Zen questioning is not psychoanalysis. While doing seated meditation, Zen practitioners keep their eyes open. The aim is awareness—full awareness—of whatever is happening in the present moment. If a memory of a deceased parent or an estranged sibling should manifest itself, it may be noted as something to look into at a later time, perhaps with the aid of a therapist. But the aim of the practice is to be mindful of whatever is happening, not to analyze or pursue the images that arise.

Toward that end, Zen questioning focuses less on specific thoughts or feelings than on the conditions that have caused them to arise. Thich Nhat Hanh, the Vietnamese Zen master, urges us to ask the question, "What am I doing?" as a way of awakening awareness of our states of mind. Barry Briggs, a teacher in the Korean Zen tradition, asks himself periodically, "How is it, just now?" By asking such questions, we can become fully aware of the concrete circumstances in which our abstract thoughts are occurring. And we can discern whether the thought we're having, the remark we're about to make, or the action we're about to take is habitual or fresh, reflexive or wisely responsive.

Beyond these practical modes of self-interrogation, Zen questioning is also a process of radical, unmediated inquiry. "Who hears the sound?" asked the fourteenth-century Zen master Bassui Tokushō. It is a question to be asked, over and again, in a spirit of not-knowing, until the truth of the self is revealed with incontrovertible clarity. "What is *this*?" Bassui also asked, demanding a fearless, unrelenting inquiry into the nature of reality. Norman Fischer has likened such questioning to a torch, which burns away "all the dross and scum of desire and confusion that covers ordinary activities."

Zen questioning is hard—harder, said Shunryu Suzuki, than giving up smoking. But its aim is a life no longer governed by fear, anger, habit, or forgetfulness, and it is well worth the effort.

February 18, 2010

Dappled Things

"Glory be to God," wrote the poet-priest Gerard Manley Hopkins, "for dappled things. / For skies of couple-color as a brinded cow." An archaic form of "brindled," "brinded" means "streaked" or "having patches of a darker hue." Couple-colored skies are at once dark and light. Other dappled things, as seen by Hopkins, include "finches' wings," "rose-moles all in stipple upon trout that swim," and "all trades, their gear and tackle and trim." All are parts of the interdependent body of reality, and all are included in Hopkins's vision of "pied beauty."

Zen teachings, ancient and modern, accord with Hopkins's vision. The *Heart Sutra* declares that in *sunyata*, the absolute dimension, "nothing is defiled, nothing is pure." "Defiled" and "pure" are dualistic concepts, projected by the human mind upon undifferentiated reality. Seng-ts'an's *Faith-Mind Sutra* elaborates the point, cautioning the reader against the delusions attendant to dualistic thinking. "It is due to our grasping and rejecting," writes Seng-ts'an, "that we do not know the true nature of things." Attached to our

160

preferences, our liking and disliking, we "remain in a dualistic state." However, if we can free ourselves of our attachment to "refined" and "vulgar" and other comparative concepts, we can see "the ten thousand things" just as they are. We can recognize that they are "of a single essence," and we can "walk in harmony with the nature of things, [our] own fundamental nature," freely and undisturbed.

The non-dualistic outlook articulated by Seng-ts'an may also be found in the literature of Zen, particularly its poetry. The wandering poet Matsuo Basho (1644–1694), best known for his idyllic haiku, "The old pond— / frog jumps in / sound of water," describes, in a less decorous haiku, "a fishy smell— / perch guts / in the water weeds." In yet another, he records the experience of "fleas, lice, / a horse peeing / near [his] pillow." And Gary Snyder (b.1930), a Zen practitioner and committed environmentalist, describes an "eight-petaled yellow 'Shell'" sign and a "blue-and-white 'Mobil' with a big red 'O' // growing in the asphalt riparian zone / by the soft roar of the flow / of Interstate 5." Whatever his political views, Snyder does not condemn these emblems of corporate America. On the contrary, in Snyder's vision, as in Hopkins's and Basho's, pleasant and unpleasant, refined and ugly phenomena are parts of the great, indivisible body of reality. All are worthy of regard.

So, too, are the brindled skies of our inner lives, where the "ten thousand sorrows" consort with the "ten thousand joys." Should we venture to look inward, we might well discover the counterparts of fish guts and horse piss, fleas and lice in our psyches. And if we are meditative practitioners, we might also discover traces of what the Tibetan master Trungpa Rinpoche called "spiritual materialism," by which he meant pride in spiritual achievement. Unlike Vipassana ("insight") meditation, Zen practice does not encourage inspection of the emotional subtexts of our thoughts, such as might occur in psychoanalysis, but it does encourage an open, non-judgmental awareness of the motley images that cross our minds. And ultimately, the aim of the practice is not only awareness of changing thoughts and images but also contact with "original mind," the timeless ground of being, from which those thoughts and images have sprung.

March, it might be said, is the month of dappled things. Patches of snow coexist with patches of grass, gray slush with crocuses and snowdrops. Looking out on that piebald landscape, we can wish impatiently for April and an end to winter. Or, as Hopkins did, we can appreciate the streaks of darkness and light, while also intuiting the underlying whole. Before our eyes is the changing relative world, where things are, in Hopkins's phrase, "swift, slow; sweet, sour; adazzle, dim." Beyond our eyes is absolute reality, the beginningless ground of being, whose beauty, in Hopkins's words, is "past change."

March 4, 2010

Carols, Hymns, and Chants

*L*ike forms in the natural world, musical forms have their own, distinct identities. A ballad is one thing, a sonata another. In his review of the *Cowley Carol Book* (1902), a collection of traditional Christmas carols, the British musicologist Sir William Henry Hadow (1859–1937) explores the differences between two such forms: the carol and the hymn. Although Sir Henry's discussion has nothing overtly to do with Zen, it brings to mind an important component of Zen practice.

As Sir Henry explains, a carol is the "folk-song of religious music; its essential character is simple, human, direct; it sings its message of joy and welcome, of peace and goodwill, and remembers, while it sings, the sanctity of motherhood and the gentleness of little children." Carols are by nature democratic. They appeal to emotions that are "the common heritage of mankind," and they aim at "no display of learning, no pageantry of ceremonial." They are "the service of poor men in their working garb," and they bring "tidings which all may hear and understand." In keeping with their humble origins, the melodies of carols are "simple and flow-ing" and "easy to remember." Their native place is the "open air," where a "few rude voices" are singing "under the frosty stars."

By contrast, hymns are most at home in churches and ca-thedrals. They are an instrument of worship, and they have an authorized place in the Sunday service. In their solemnity and grandeur, hymns represent the "majesty and erudition of the Church." Marked by "intricacy of contrapuntal device," "in-genuity of modulation," and "colored or perfumed harmony," hymns by the likes of William Byrd sort well with the "fretted aisles and blazoned windows" of the great English cathedrals. Unlike the carol, which evokes a beautiful "beggar-maiden" in peasant rags, the hymn wears "a sumptuous habit of jewels and brocade." It is an integral part of Anglican liturgy, and it carries the weight of ecclesiastical authority.

Zen has no exact equivalent of the hymn or carol. West-ern "bare-bones" Zen, as practiced by Toni Packer, Joan Tol-lifson, and others, dispenses with liturgy altogether; and even the liturgy of formal Zen, with its wood-blocks, bows, and bells, is a plain austere affair, at least when contrasted with Sunday morning at York Minster or Evensong at King's Col-lege, Cambridge.

Yet formal Zen does make use of chants, which combine the most prominent features of hymns and carols. Like the hymn, such chants as *Atta Dipa* ("You are the Light"), the *Heart Sutra*, and the *Four Great Vows* embody the authority of a venerable tradition. Chanted in Pali or Sino-Japanese, they evoke a strangeness comparable to that of an Anglican Mass. At the same time, most Zen chants are, in musical terms, rudimentary. The *Heart Sutra* is chanted in a rhythmic monotone, and *Atta Dipa* consists of two notes at an interval of a fourth (*do-fa*). However strange their idiom or formidable their authority, they can be learned and chanted by anyone.

Unlike its counterpart in Christian liturgy, Zen chanting is not a form of worship. Its functions are, first, to loosen the diaphragm in preparation for seated meditation, and second, to unify the body, breath, and mind in the act of chanting. As John Daido Loori Roshi has noted, Zen chanting grounds the practitioner in the here-and-now. No less important, it serves to cultivate wholesome states of mind, particularly those of respect and gratitude. In Daido Roshi's words, Zen chanting has "little to do with the volume of your voice. It has all to do with the state of your mind."

Nowhere are these purposes more evident than in *Tei Dai Denpo*, or lineage chanting, in which Zen practitioners intone the names of their ancestral teachers. *Shido Bunan Zenji. Dokyo Etan Zenji. Hakuin Ekaku Zenji* ... Echoing in the *zendo*, this ancient chant evokes a mood of profound communal gratitude. Traversing the centuries, it conjures an unbroken lineage of practice, thought, and feeling, extending from the fifth century B.C.E. to the present day. An amalgam, if you like, of hymn and carol, it also honors the teachers in ourselves.

March 18, 2010

CB's List

"**D**eath is certain," Zen teachings remind us, "but the time of death is uncertain." What truth could be more evident, one might say, what reality more apparent. And yet that truth and that reality are difficult to accept, even under the most auspicious conditions. And should we learn that our own death is imminent, the difficulty increases a hundred fold.

So it was with Carol Ruth Burdick (1928–2008), my friend of forty years, who learned on the evening of Friday, February 29, 2008 that she had advanced pancreatic cancer. Known to her community as "CB," Carol was seventy-nine years old. Surgery, as she saw it, was out of the question, as was chemotherapy. The plain fact was that she was going to die, and soon. Rather than share that fact with friends or family, she spent the night facing it alone.

Knowing nothing of her diagnosis, I called CB early the next morning to inquire after her health and to suggest that we meet for conversation, as we often did on Saturday mornings. When she told me her bad news, I expressed my sympathy, but I didn't know what to say. "What's the prognosis?" I asked.

"About six weeks," she replied.

A few hours later, CB and I sat at her dining-room table, looking out of her big picture window at her frozen pond. Her mood seemed preternaturally calm. "How are you feeling?" I asked. In response, she reported that during the night she had made a list of the ten "positive aspects" of her impending death. "You know how I hate positive thinking," she declared—and then went on to read her list.

First, she would not be a burden to her grown children. Second, she would not suffer the humiliation of senile dementia. Third, she would not become destitute. Fourth, she would not have to endure a second knee replacement. Fifth, she would no longer need to worry about her internal pains, for now she knew their cause. Her list continued, each item detailing another benefit of her death—silver linings, if you like, in the darkest of clouds.

Exactly six weeks later, on another Saturday morning, CB passed away. Since then, I've often thought of her list. What prompted her to compose it, I've wondered, and what purpose did it serve?

To some, CB's list might seem an elaborate form of denial, a rationalist's defense against an implacable force. Perhaps it was, but I would prefer to see it as an expression of her literary sensibility and her practical outlook. CB was a published writer of poems and essays, articles and memoirs. It was natural that she would turn to language and literary form to articulate her situation. And CB was also an unsparing realist, who cast a cold eye on human folly and romantic self-deception. Void of such notions as a happy afterlife or a lasting legacy, her list acknowledged the concrete changes her death would bring, both for herself and her loved ones. It was not a wish list but a sober appraisal, reflective of both her stern Protestant upbringing and her literary education.

Yet CB's list was more than a realist's analysis. It was also, in its way, an affirmation of the wholeness of life. *Positive/negative*; *good/bad*; *fortunate/unfortunate*: by their very nature, such dualities divide the stream of being into artificial halves, favoring one over the other and falsifying the whole. Perhaps that's why CB disliked "positive thinking," which not only "accentuates the positive," as the old show tune advises us to do, but also isolates half of our experience at the expense of the other. And perhaps that's also why CB fashioned her list, which redressed the balance of darkness and light, sadness and happiness in her present experience. For her family and friends as well as herself, her list afforded honest consolation. Beyond that, it affirmed the unity of life and death, creation and destruction, even in the midst of loss. Sober though it was, her list was a hymn to life *and* death, a lapsed Protestant's *L'Chaim*.

Carol Burdick was Adjunct Professor of English at Alfred University and the author of *Haps & Mishaps: Sketches from a Rural Life* (Whitlock Publishing, 2008).

April 1, 2010

Leaving Things Alone

"Ah, she was a terror for the flowers," an Irish widower once remarked of his late wife. "She had no gift for leaving things alone."

Few of us Westerners do, including those of us who practice Zen meditation. "Zazen," writes the Soto master Kosho Uchiyama Roshi, "enables life to be life by letting it be." And Shunryu Suzuki Roshi, author of *Zen Mind, Beginner's Mind*, advises us to "let things go as they go." But how, exactly, are we to do that when practicing seated meditation? How much, if any, control should we relinquish, and when?

Nearly all the manuals agree that the Zen practitioner should sit in a stable posture, knees down and spine erect, and pay attention to the breath. But should we regulate our breathing? Should we count our breaths or simply observe the flow of air as it comes and goes? Is it really necessary to hold our hands in the "cosmic mudra," left palm resting in the right? Should we strive to silence our inner chatter— or allow it to continue? Answers to these questions may be found, but they vary according to the school and the teacher.

Among those who advocate stern control, Japanese Rinzai masters occupy a pre-eminent position. Rinzai Zen has been likened to a "brave general who moves a regiment without delay," and with few exceptions Rinzai teachers live up to that description. The renowned Rinzai master Omori Sogen Roshi advises the student to push the breath into the lower abdomen and "squeeze it lightly there with a scooping feeling." Katsuki Sekida, another Rinzai teacher, directs the practitioner to narrow the exhalation by "holding the diaphragm down and steadily checking the upward pushing movement of the abdominal muscles." Similar admonitions regarding breath, posture, and concentration resound throughout the Rinzai literature, lending a tone of rigorous authority.

By contrast, Soto Zen takes a less severe approach, urging continuous awareness more than strict control. Soto teachers do emphasize form in general and correct posture in particular, but the intent is less to marshal the body into submission than to facilitate the open flow of breath and the cultivation of awareness. In his *Opening the Hand of Thought*, Uchiyama Roshi admonishes us just to "drop everything and entrust everything to the correct zazen posture." In similar fashion, he instructs us not to suppress discursive thoughts but merely to let go of "all the accidental things that rise in our minds." Firm but gentle, Uchiyama's instructions typify Soto teachings, which have been likened to a "farmer taking care of a rice field, one stalk after another, patiently."

At the least directive end of the spectrum, the non-traditional teacher Toni Packer advocates "fresh seeing" but no particular control of breath or posture. In her essay "A Few Tips for Sitting," she offers this advice:

No need to be rigid about proper posture. The back lifts itself up spontaneously as the mind inquires, opens up, and empties out. It is intimately related to our varying states of mind. In experiencing pain, sorrow, anger, fear, or greed, the body manifests each mood in its own ways. In openness and clarity the body feels like no-body.

Like those poets who view literary form as an "extension" (or revelation) of content, Packer views proper posture not as a form to be externally imposed but as an expression of an open, inquiring state of mind.

To the newcomer, the rich variety of methods that marks Western Zen can be more bewildering than encouraging. Whom should you trust, and what method should you follow? As a general rule, the unaffiliated novice would do well to choose a method and stay with it long enough to determine whether the prescribed forms of control promote or detract from the development of awareness. For my own part, I often begin a sitting with the Rinzai practice of *susokkan*, or counting of out-breaths. Later on in the sitting, I practice *zuisokukan*, or following the breath, focusing on the lower abdomen. Toward the end, I settle into *shikantaza*, or "just sitting," which is sometimes called the "method of no method." Although this sequence will not suit everyone, I have found it a skillful means for gradually relinquishing control. At the outset of the sitting I am, as it were, making something happen. By the end, I am learning, in the manner of the Taoist master Chuang Tzu, to "gaze at the world but leave the world alone."

April 15, 2010

The Sword of Attention

Many years ago, when my son was still in diapers and I was a new and inexperienced father, I spoke with a visiting poet about the challenges of fatherhood. Among them was the challenge of pushing a diaper pin through several layers of cloth without sticking it into my son.

Gray-haired and world-weary, the poet was himself the father of four grown children. "With our firstborn," he reflected, "I used to worry about that. But by the time the fourth one came along, I just pushed the pin in and hoped for the best."

I suspect that the poet was exaggerating, or tailoring his reflection for comic effect. But his remark has proved memorable, perhaps because it illustrates the degree to which second, third, and fourth experiences differ from the first. The first time around, we may be fully attentive, whether out of fear or wonder or concern. By the fourth, we may be indifferent or complacent. What once was fresh has become old hat.

To restore our initial wonder is a central aim of Zen practice. What Shunryu Suzuki Roshi famously called beginner's mind is no other than the capacity to experience the world freely and openly, without prior judgments or self-centered agendas. In *Zen Mind, Beginner's Mind*, he puts it this way:

> *Our "original mind" includes everything within itself. It is always rich and sufficient within itself. You should not lose your self-sufficient state of mind. This does not mean a closed mind, but actually an empty and a ready mind. If your mind is empty, it is ready for anything; it is open to everything. In the beginner's mind there are many possibilities; in the expert's mind there are few.*

Meeting the world with "original mind," we bring a receptive awareness to whatever we encounter, holding our memories and preconceptions in abeyance. Original mind, Suzuki goes on to say, is the mind of boundless compassion. To return to original mind is to open ourselves not only to our immediate surroundings but also to the interdependent, ever-changing web of life.

But how is one to do that? By what means are we to meet the fourth—or five hundredth—experience of a repeated action with "original mind"?

In her book *Everyday Zen*, Charlotte Joko Beck offers this advice:

> *A zendo is not a place for bliss and relaxation, but a furnace room for the combustion of our egoistic delusions. What tools do we need to use? Only one. We've all heard of it, yet we use it very seldom. It's called* attention.

> *Attention is the cutting, burning sword, and our prac-*
> *tice is to use that sword as much as we can. None of us*
> *is very willing to use it; but when we do—even for a few*
> *minutes—some cutting and burning takes place. All prac-*
> *tice aims to increase our ability to be attentive, not just in*
> *zazen but in every moment of our life.*

What the burning sword cuts through, Beck subsequently explains, is delusive conceptual thought. By paying close and continuous attention, we come to realize that "the conceptual process is a fantasy; and the more we grasp this the more our ability to pay attention to reality increases."

Egoistic delusions are many, but few are more pervasive or potentially harmful than the illusion of sufficient expertise: of already knowing it all, or all that is relevant to the occasion. Whether the activity be pinning a diaper or chopping an onion, managing a portfolio or diagnosing an illness, the "expert's mind" may well be closed to possibilities. It may also misperceive the facts, jump to conclusions, or ignore conflicting evidence. Cutting through the self-centered concept of expertise, the sword of attention clears a path to the unknown, unprecedented reality before us. Burning away conceptions and misconceptions, prejudices and expectations, it enables us to encounter the present moment on its own terms rather than impose our own. "Don't-Know Mind," the Korean master Seung Sahn liked to call it. "Only don't know!" Difficult to cultivate and even more difficult to maintain, it is essential to the practice of Zen.

April 29, 2010

To Study the Self

*I*magine, if you will, that you are walking down the sidewalk on a bright May morning. The air feels fresh and warm. As you walk along, you notice the new leaves on the trees, the yellow dandelions dotting the green lawns. And as you take note of the external world, you also become aware of yourself moving through that world.

It occurs to you that you are a member of a community—a solid citizen, one might say. But you are also an independent self, separate and apart from your human and natural environment. In your wallet you have an ID, and at home a birth certificate. You may also have degrees or diplomas, a lengthy resume, a record of achievement. Certainly you have your special talents and acquired skills, and you also have your preferences—wine over beer, perhaps, or neither if you are a teetotaler. Where personal finances are concerned, you are better off than many, though far inferior, socially and financially, to the celebrities you see on TV. In any event, you are separate from and superior to the toads, frogs, and other creatures of the natural world, not to mention the plants and minerals. Were you to liken yourself to a non-human object, it might be a late-model car—a Prius, perhaps, or a Ford Focus. Sadly, that vehicle will one day end up in the salvage yard, but for now it's running fine.

Now consider your self from another angle. Although you might prefer to see yourself as an independent entity, separate from your human and natural surroundings, you are in actuality as porous as a sponge. If the weather were damp and cold, you might not be feeling so cheerful. Were the flowers withered or beaten down, you might feel the same. And not only your mood but the very existence of your "self" depends on "non-self" elements: the sunlight warming your face, the water flowing in the water mains, the breakfast settling in your stomach. Moreover, not even one of your vaunted attainments would have been possible without the support of other people: not your projects and awards, your commendations or your cherished possessions. Were you to examine your place in the cosmos, you might liken yourself to a wave, which other waves have created and sustained.

Such are the contrasting perspectives in which the construct known as a "self" might be perceived and understood. If the first perspective is initially the more comforting, it is perhaps because it reflects a familiar, common-sense view of reality. In Zen teachings, this viewpoint is known as "ordinary mind," and its frame of reference is the "relative" (or "historical") dimension of our experience. In the relative dimension, up is up, and down is down. Self is one thing, non-self another.

Yet to those who are living on the other side of our planet, what we call up is down. And from the standpoint of absolute reality, which in Zen is known as the "ultimate dimension," conceptual dualities such as "up" and "down," "self" and "non-self," are viewed as necessary but insubstantial. To exist at all, "up" needs "down." Similarly, "self" and "non-self" are interdependent parts of an indivisible whole. As Zen master Thich Nhat Hanh reminds us, a flower is made of "non-flower" elements: light, soil, water, and so forth. Without them, the flower could not be. And what is true of the flower is also true of us. Without sunlight, water, food, and other people, none of us could live, or live in good health, for very long. What appear in the relative dimension to be separate entities—self and other, human and non-human beings—are, in the ultimate dimension, parts of the one, interconnected body of reality, where everything is changing, and everything depends on everything else.

To contrast these two perspectives is not to suggest that the first is false and the second true, the one benighted and the other enlightened. Rather, it is to propose that if we are to stay in touch with reality, and to live in harmony with reality, both perspectives must be kept in mind. "To study the Way" wrote Eihei Dogen, founder of the Soto Zen tradition, "is to study the self. To study the self is to forget the self. And to forget the self is to awaken to the ten thousand things."

May 13, 2010

From Rouge to the Color of Moonlight

On Thursday, May 6, 2010, the Dow-Jones Industrial Average dropped nearly a thousand points in less than an hour. By the end of the day, the Dow had bounced back up to record a net loss of 348 points. On that same day, British voters went to the polls, and the next morning we learned that Britain had created its first "hung parliament" since the 1970s, exposing America's closest ally to new uncertainties.

Observing these changes and others like them, I'm reminded of the word *rely*, whose root meaning is "to bind" or "to fasten"—a root it shares with the word *religion*. Whether the context be financial, religious, or personal, on what if anything should we fasten our trust? On what should we rely?

"Some have relied on what they knew," writes Robert Frost in "Provide, Provide," a poem about old age, "Others on simply being true. / What worked for them might work for you." Perhaps it might, but the realist Frost, who knows that "[t]oo many fall from great and good / For you to doubt the likelihood," is not convinced. "Make the whole stock exchange your own!" he urges the chastened reader. And in his closing stanza he offers this advice:

> Better to go down dignified
> With boughten friendship at your side
> Than none at all. Provide, provide!

In New England dialect, "boughten" means "purchased." If you have indeed provided for a wealthy retirement, you can bribe your greedy friends to surround your deathbed. Better them than no one.

At about the same time as Frost was writing "Provide, Provide," the Japanese poet Miyazawa Kenji composed these lines:

> In the world of these phenomena
> where everything is unreliable,
> where you cannot count on anything,
> the unreliable attributes
> help form such a beautiful raindrop
> and dye a warped spindle tree
> like a gorgeous fabric
> from rouge to the color of moonlight.

Like Frost, Miyazawa recognizes the unreliability of the world. Unlike Frost, however, he views the "unreliable attributes" of the natural world as the basis of natural beauty. Undependable though they are, those shifting conditions create the beauty of the raindrop and the gorgeous, changing colors of the spindle tree.

The *Diamond-Cutter Sutra*, a core text for Zen practitioners, offers yet another perspective. In one of the most celebrated passages of that sutra, the listener who would become a Bodhisattva (an enlightened being) is admonished to develop "a pure, lucid mind that doesn't depend upon sight, sound, touch, flavor, smell, or any thought that arises in it." He or she should cultivate a "mind that alights nowhere." According to legend, the peasant boy Hui-Neng, who would later become the Sixth Ancestor of the Zen tradition, experienced awakening upon hearing monks recite that passage in the marketplace.

But what does it mean to develop "a mind that alights nowhere"? The Buddhist scholar Mu Soeng understands the original phrase to mean "a mind that is free from any kind of clinging." It binds to nothing. However, Zen master Thich Nhat Hanh, using a different translation, interprets the passage to mean "that mind that is not caught up in anything." Such a mind does not get caught up in the objects of the five senses because all such objects are "conditioned and constantly changing." They are unstable and not to be relied upon.

What, then, are we to rely upon? As Thich Nhat Hanh points out, there are many stable things upon which to depend—the earth and the air, for example. But the most stable is "to abide in the non-abiding," which is to say, to return through the practice of meditation to absolute reality, the ground of being, from which all conditioned phenomena, including the fluctuations of the stock market and the changing colors of the spindle tree, are constantly arising. Like the wave that rises from the water, only to return, the uncertain, fearful mind can return to immovable awareness, finding a place to rest and a source on which to rely.

May 27, 2010

Batter Up

On Saturday, August 4, 2007, Alex Rodriguez hit his 500th home run. When *Elvis left the building*, as sportscasters sometimes say, the thirty-two-year-old Rodriguez became the youngest player to join the 500 Club. He also became the third player to do so while wearing a Yankees uniform, the previous two being Mickey Mantle and Babe Ruth.

However momentous A-Rod's achievement—the ball he drove into the left-field seats later sold for more than $100,000—it was not brought about by an act of will. On the contrary, his fervent desire to hit one more homer had stood in his way. On July 25 Rodriguez had hit his 499th home run at Kansas City. With expectations rising to a frenzy, he had tried through the next five games to hit his 500th, adapting his swing for that purpose. Only when he returned to his regular swing, trying only to hit hard, was he able to succeed. "I've conceded the fact," he said afterward, "that you can't will yourself to hit a home run."

In Zen practice, the counterpart of a home run in baseball is the experience of *kensho*, which means "seeing into one's true nature." Kensho arises from two primary conditions, the first being "accumulated *samadhi*"—rigorous meditative training—and the second a "triggering event," such as the sight of a falling leaf or the sound of a stone striking bamboo. In kensho, the practitioner experiences a dramatic falling away of the personal ego and a profound sense of unity with all things. Of the many accounts of kensho in Zen literature, one of the most vivid is that of Peter Matthiessen, who experienced it while training at Dai Bosatsu Zendo:

> *And very suddenly, on an inhaled breath, this earthbound body-mind, in a great hush, began to swell and fragment and dissolve in light, expanding outward into a fresh universe in the very process of creation*
>
> *At the bell ending the period, I fell back into my body. Yet those clear moments had been an* experience *that everything was right-here-now, contained in "me."*

With this experience came laughter, then weeping, then "a spontaneous rush of love for friends, family, and children, for all the beings striving in this room, for every one and every thing, without distinction."

Given its prominence in Zen lore, particularly in the Rinzai school of Zen, the experience of kensho can easily become a goal of the Zen practitioner. If he or she can just attain that experience, the long and often painful hours of sitting will be vindicated. Yet if there is one thing Zen teachings, Soto and Rinzai alike, agree upon, it is that striving to experience kensho only undermines one's practice and defeats its purpose. In the words of the Soto master Kosho Uchiyama, "to think that people become great by doing zazen, or to think that you are going to *gain* satori, is to be sadly misled by your own illusion." Or, as the Korean master Seung Sahn memorably puts it, "wanting enlightenment is a big mistake."

What, then, is one to do? In his book *Zen Action, Zen Person*, T.P. Kasulis likens the longtime Zen practitioner to a seasoned batter at the plate:

> *Although the novice is always thinking about what he or she is doing while doing it (left shoulder down, eye on the ball, shifting weight to the front leg), the accomplished player, once readied in the batter's box, ceases such dualistic thoughts and becomes purely reactive. Hinging total awareness on the pivotal moment we call the present, he or she merely waits, poised to respond to the virtually infinite number of paths the ball might travel.*

And Tetsugen Bernie Glassman, an American Zen master, has this to say about kensho:

> *I think kensho is essential*—it has to happen. *And so long as the practice is constant and steady, so long as the student continues to practice without being intent on* achieving *some "special" state, something that he or she has heard about, it will. When that idea of gain falls away, people open up.*

What these statements together suggest, and what centuries of practitioners have confirmed, is that if we commit ourselves to the daily practice of zazen, without a "gaining idea," we will not only quiet our minds and ready ourselves for whatever life might throw our way. We might also find, in some future hour, that Elvis has left the building.

June 10, 2010

Saying Nothing

*E*arly one morning, a friend of mine ventured to compliment his wife, who was sitting upright in bed. "You look lovely today," he noted.

"Only today?" she replied.

My friend might learn two lessons from this experience. The first is ably expressed by a character in one of the Irish writer Claire Keegan's stories. "Many's the man," he reflects, "lost much just because he missed a perfect opportunity to say nothing."

The second lesson is that the English language is inherently dualistic. "Today" in this instance is an adverb, indicating when an action occurred. *Today* is not yesterday and not tomorrow. By implication, if not by overt statement, my friend excluded those other possibilities.

Applying this principle to the word "holiness," Thich Nhat Hanh offers this observation:

Holiness is only the word "holiness." And when we say the word "holiness," we eliminate everything that isn't holy,

*like the ordinary. If there is no ordinary, how can there be
holiness? Therefore any words, even words like "holiness,"
"beautiful," and "Buddha," eliminate part of the true nature of the thing in describing it. ... When we say a name
out loud, it is as if we are slashing a knife into reality and
cutting it into small pieces.*

In Zen teachings, the act of slashing reality into small
pieces is called discrimination, and the mind that performs
this act is the discriminating mind, which distinguishes self
from other and *this* from *that*. Employing dualistic language
to that end, the discriminating mind might say that someone
is an "acquaintance" rather than a "friend," implying that the
same person cannot be both. Or, to view it the other way
round, by employing language in the first place, the mind is
led to discriminate, since language itself discriminates, elimi-
nating part of what it purports to describe. To say that someone is an acquaintance is to think, or to lead oneself to think,
that he or she is not a friend.

Dualistic language also generates opinion. The language
may be minimal, as when women express their opinion of
"men" simply by saying the word. Or it may be elaborate,
as when Oscar Wilde observes that "all women become like
their mothers. That's their tragedy. No man does. That's his."
But whether the expression be simple or complex, direct or
ironic, personal opinion and dualistic language are of a piece,
each serving to reinforce the other.

The American poet Jane Hirshfield, a longtime Zen practitioner, acknowledges as much in her poem "To Opinion,"
in which she addresses Opinion as though it were a sentient
being. Positing that a capacity to have opinions is what de-

fines the human, she notes that "a mosquito's estimation of her meal, however subtle, / is not an opinion." She also recognizes that to think about Opinion is to have one. It is to "step into" something (*"your arms? a thicket? pitfall?"*) Most poignantly, when she senses Opinion "rising strongly" in her, she feels herself "grow separate / and more lonely." Opinions divide people, not only from others but from the wholeness of their own experience. And language—the poet's medium—is both the source and the instrument of Opinion.

What, then, is one to do? Hirshfield recalls a line from the Japanese poet Myoe—*Bright, bright, bright, bright, the moon*— as if to suggest that by simply repeating a word we might honor the presence of an object, rather than slash its reality into pieces. And in her closing lines, she offers an instance of her own, as she recalls a few brief minutes when Opinion "released her," and "[o]*cean ocean ocean* was the sound the sand / made of the moonlit waves / breaking on it." Rather than generate an opinion, or divide self from other, the act of repeating a mimetic name drew her closer to the natural world.

By such means, the dualistic character of language may sometimes be transcended. The self's isolation may be overcome. But should those means fail, there is another option, which is to listen rather than speak: to say nothing rather than something. In one of his many reflections on language and silence, the Trappist monk Thomas Merton entertains that possibility:

> *No writing on the solitary, meditative dimensions of life can say anything that has not already been said better by the wind in the pine trees. These pages seek nothing more than to echo the silence and peace that is "heard" when*

the rain wanders freely among the hills and forests. But what can the wind say where there is no hearer? There is then a deeper silence: the silence in which the Hearer is No-Hearer. That deeper silence must be heard before one can speak truly of solitude.

Eloquent though they are, these sentences evoke the wisdom of saying nothing.

June 24, 2010

Here and There

*B*ob Dylan once remarked that when Tommy Makem sang, there was an elsewhere in his eyes. From that elsewhere came his singing. What was true of Tommy Makem (1932–2007), the celebrated singer and songwriter from Co. Armagh, is also true of Irish balladry in general, particularly its immigrant ballads. One of the best-known ballads, Frank Fahy's version of *Galway Bay,* recalls the rugged rocks and the sweet green grass of Galway from the vantage point of Illinois. And one of the most poignant, *Sliabh Gallion Brae*, is a kind of elegy in advance, in which a farmer by the name of Joe McGarvey from Derrygenard, who can no longer pay his rent, bids farewell to the parish of Lissan, the cross of Ballinascreen, and "bonny, bonny Sliabh Gallion Brae." All are soon to be elsewhere. In the Irish language, *sliabh* (pronounced *shleeve*) means mountain, and in Scots Gaelic *brae* means hillside. As so often in immigrant ballads, an elsewhere fondly remembered is evoked through its place name, which brings its felt presence into the foreground.

To wish to be elsewhere is a universal human desire. And to become aware of that desire, even as it is arising, is one of the aims of Zen practice. Sometimes the "elsewhere" is a geographical place, as in the immigrant ballads, but just as often it is an imagined state of mind, and it lies in the future rather than the past. In her book *Nothing Special* the Zen teacher Charlotte Joko Beck examines this recurrent human impulse, as embodied in ordinary thought:

> *In ordinary thinking, the mind always has an objective, something it's going to get. If we're caught in that wanting, then our awareness of reality is gone. We've substituted a personal dream for awareness. Awareness doesn't move, doesn't bury itself in dreams; it just stays as it is.*

Ordinary thinking, as here portrayed, removes us from wherever we are. By contrast, immovable awareness grounds us in the here and now. To bring meditative awareness to our thoughts is to realize how often they serve to transport us elsewhere.

Of course, not *all* thoughts serve that purpose. *Happy to be Here*, the title of one of Garrison Keillor's books, expresses a thought that many of us have when conversing with friends at a dinner party, or spending time with a son or daughter, or eating a bowl of ice cream on a summer evening. Yet the fact is that only a few of our thoughts amplify or clarify our present experience, and many have the opposite effect. If you would like to test this claim, may I suggest that you sit still for three minutes and count the number of thoughts you have during that time. Then sit still for another three minutes, labeling your thoughts ("Thinking about tomorrow's meeting:"; "thinking about last night"). You may well find that the bulk of your thoughts pertain not to the present but to the past or the future: to where you have been or where you might sometime be. Others may pertain to no place at all, being generalized, abstract, and void of concrete particulars.

The point of this exercise is not to extinguish all such thoughts. To think about other times and places is a natural human activity, and it can give rise to artistic works as richly diverse as Billy Collins's poems on his childhood or Tommy Makem's *Farewell to Carlingford*. The point is rather to become aware of conceptual thinking and to see how it comes between our minds and the realities of our lives, bringing anxiety and untold suffering in its wake. "On the whole," W.C. Fields is thought to have written as his epitaph, "I'd rather be in Philadelphia." That makes for a good story, but like many a colorful tale, it isn't true. The real epitaph reads simply, "W.C Fields, 1880–1946." So it is with our images and thoughts, which purport to illuminate reality but often take us elsewhere.

July 8, 2010

Closing the Gap

*A*t one of the climactic moments in Shakespeare's tragedy *King Lear*, the aged king experiences a pivotal awakening. Divested of his kingdom and his power, his regal robes and loyal retinue, he finds himself on a barren heath amidst a ferocious storm. Reduced to rags himself, he sees the suffering of the indigent as never before. In a passionate soliloquy he expresses his realization:

> *Poor naked wretches, whereso'er you are,*
> *That bide the pelting of this pitiless storm,*
> *How shall your houseless heads and unfed sides,*
> *Your loop'd and windowed raggedness, defend you*
> *From seasons such as these? O, I have ta'en*
> *Too little care of this! Take physic, pomp;*
> *Expose thyself to feel what wretches feel,*
> *That thou mayst shake the superflux to them*
> *And show the heavens more just.*
>
> — III, 4

Forty-five years ago, I memorized those lines, and in four ensuing decades they have often surfaced in my awareness. Their staying power has something to do with their formal beauty, their muscular syntax and resonant pentameters. What makes this soliloquy memorable, however, is not only its forceful rhetoric but also the motive behind it: that of a fallen king, who has realized at long last that he must dissolve the barriers between himself and the suffering of others. He must take "physic" (medicine) to cure the illness of pomposity, the sickness of class prejudice. He must close the gap between himself and others' suffering.

That is also a motive of Zen practice, whose ultimate aims are the relief of suffering and the cultivation of compassionate wisdom. From the vantage point of Zen teachings, the notion of a separate self is an illusion, whether that self be a king or a homeless serf. And that illusion causes suffering, both to the king and the serf: the subject and object in a mutual relationship. For the reality is that we are all enmeshed in what Martin Luther King, Jr. called an "inescapable network of mutuality, tied into a single garment of destiny." To deny that reality is to live in a self-centered dream—and to widen the gap between self and other.

But how, in practice, is one to close that gap? Short of becoming destitute and desperate ourselves, how are we to awaken, fully and compassionately, to others' suffering?

For the Zen practitioner, the best medicine is meditation, which not only steadies the mind but also affords access to our internal suffering and its causes. To attend to others' suffering, Zen teachings tell us, we must first attend to our own. This directive is not a prescription for self-pity or an invitation to wallow in our woes. Rather, it is an admonition to become aware of the elements in our psyches and our culture that engender suffering—the craving, fear, and anger; the impulse to violence; the mindless consumption; the habitual patterns of reactivity. Only when we have gained insight into these forces and, if possible, transformed them into something more constructive, will we be in a position to pay full attention to others' distress, much less help to relieve it. As Thich Nhat Hanh sternly puts it, "we have to dissolve all prejudices, barriers, and walls and empty ourselves in order to listen and look deeply before we utter even one word." If we can manage that daunting task, we will be in a far better position to act for the benefit of others.

What we will do will depend on the circumstances. It might be humanitarian action, but it might also be the act of stopping and listening, wholeheartedly and without preconceptions, to those with whom we engage in everyday life. Thich Nhat Hanh calls this practice "deep listening," by which he means unprejudiced, non-judgmental attention to another person's suffering. "Deep listening and loving speech," he writes, "are wonderful instruments to help us arrive at the kind of understanding we all need as a basis for appropriate action. You listen deeply for only one purpose—to allow the other person to empty his or her heart. This is already an act of relieving suffering."

By such means, any one of us might close the gap—and show the heavens more just.

July 22, 2010

Pursuing the Real

When greyhounds race on a track, they chase an artificial rabbit. Mistaking that furry object for the real thing, they pursue it with all their might.

During a recent greyhound race in Australia, however, a living, breathing rabbit wandered onto the track. Spotting that hapless creature, a greyhound named Ginny Lou took off in hot pursuit, leaving the other dogs to their delusion. Apparently, Ginny Lou could distinguish between the illusory and the real, and she chose to pursue the latter.

To make that distinction is also the work of the Zen practitioner. And to reconnect us with our actual lives is a defining aim of Zen meditation. The poet Czeslaw Milosz once described the art of poetry as the "passionate pursuit of the Real," and much the same might be said of Zen practice. During the course of a day we might expend the bulk of our energy chasing artificial rabbits, but when we are practicing Zen meditation, we are pursuing the real one: the moment-to-moment reality of things as they are.

That pursuit often begins with the body. The *Sutra on the Full Awareness of Breathing*, a foundational text for Zen students, directs the practitioner to recite, "Breathing in, I am aware of my body // Breathing out, I calm my body." In keeping with that prescription, the contemporary Zen teacher Zoketsu Norman Fischer advises us to begin a sitting by sweeping our awareness lightly through our bodies. "The point," he explains, "is to arrive in the body, to be aware of the body as sensation and process, to ground [ourselves] in the body as basis so that thought and emotion don't fly too far afield." In similar fashion, Zen master Thich Nhat Hanh directs us to bring compassionate awareness to the various parts of our bodies, including our internal organs: "Aware of my lungs, I breathe in. / Smiling to my lungs, I breathe out. / Aware of my heart, I breathe in. / Bringing kind attention to my heart, I breathe out." By such means, we return to our bodies, grounding ourselves in our physical lives.

Having established ourselves in that awareness, we can then turn our attention to our states of mind. In Zen teachings, mind and body are often seen as aspects of each other. "What happens to the body," Thich Nhat Hanh reminds us, "happens to the mind." By being aware of the present state of the body—relaxed or tense, energetic or fatigued, balanced or imbalanced—we may already be aware of our present state of mind. To sharpen that awareness, however, we might ask ourselves, "What is my state of mind just now?" Or, more concretely, "Is my mind/body tight or loose?" Employing that classic analogy (which originally referred to the strings of a lute), we can then investigate the causes of tightness or looseness, identifying such specific states as craving, fear, or anger, on the one hand, or balance, elation, and equanimity, on the other. And as with awareness of the body, we can bring kind attention to whatever state of mind we may be experiencing, noting the effect of our awareness on our fear or anger, our craving or agitation.

Meditation of this kind steadies the body and mind. In Zen practice, however, it also serves a broader aim, which is the recognition and acceptance of our present lives, just as they are, just now. "Do not get carried away," Dogen Zenji admonishes us in his *Instructions to the Cook*, "by the sounds of spring, nor become heavy-hearted upon seeing the colors of fall. View the changes of the seasons as a whole, and weigh the relativeness of light and heavy from a broad perspective." Commenting on this passage, the Soto master Kosho Uchiyama urges us "to be resolved that whatever we meet *is* our life," and to "see the four seasons of favorable circumstances, adversity, despair, and exaltation all as the scenery of [our lives]." Such an attitude, which Dogen identifies as "Magnanimous Mind," can profoundly alter our experience of the world, engendering a deeper realism as well as a more balanced perspective. Uchiyama Roshi describes its impact in this way:

> When we have developed this kind of attitude toward our lives, the meaning of living day by day changes completely, along with our valuation of the events and people and circumstances that arise. Since we no longer try to escape from delusion, misfortune, or adversity, nor chase after enlightenment and peace of mind, things like money and position lose their former value. People's reputations or their skills at maneuvering in society have no bearing on the way we see them as human beings, nor does a certificate of

enlightenment make any impression on anyone. What is primary and essential is that as we develop this vision, the meaning of encountering the things, situations, or people in our lives completely changes.

Artificial rabbits abound, as do encouragements to chase them. But as Dogen's observations and Uchiyama's commentary make clear, we can indeed develop another kind of vision, in which things appear as they actually are, not as our conditioning would have them be. Like Ginny Lou, we too can pursue the real.

August 19, 2010

Back to School

*T*his is the season when students go back to school. Here in Alfred, New York, the college students have already returned, and the yellow buses will soon be rolling again. There is a youthful freshness in the air.

Zen students also go back to school, but that action occurs with each new sitting, each fresh encounter with things as they are. Shunryu Suzuki Roshi describes the process in this way:

> *Once in a while you should stop all your activities and make your screen white. That is zazen. That is the foundation of our everyday life and our meditation practice. Without this kind of foundation your practice will not work. All the instructions you receive are about how to have a clean white screen, even though it is never pure white because of various attachments and previous stains.*

The clean white screen to which Suzuki Roshi refers is a mind without prejudice or expectations, judgments or rigid notions. In the Zen practice of *shikantaza*, or "just sitting," the mind of the practitioner becomes the mental counter-part of a clean new notebook—or what, in grade school, we used to call our tablets. Open and unmarked, such a mind is ready to receive whatever comes its way.

Yet, as Suzuki observes, the screen is not pure white. At-tachments and stains prevent our minds from being immacu-late or entirely open. Prominent among those attachments is our fear of the unknown and our expectation, conscious or otherwise, that whatever we encounter should fit our pre-conceptions. And prominent among the stains is our previ-ous knowledge, which ought to help us interpret experience but often has the opposite effect.

Commenting on what Zen calls "the barrier built of knowledge," Zen master Thich Nhat Hanh distinguishes be-tween mere knowledge and true understanding:

> Old knowledge is the obstacle to new understanding. ...
> Like those who are awakened, great scientists have under-gone great internal changes. If they are able to achieve pro-found realization, it is because their powers of observation, concentration, and awareness are deeply developed.
>
> Understanding is not an accumulation of knowledge. To the contrary, it is the result of the struggle to become free of knowledge. Understanding shatters old knowledge to make room for the new that accords better with reality. When Copernicus discovered that the Earth goes around the sun, most of the astronomical knowledge of the time had to be discarded, including the ideas of above and be-low. Today, physics is struggling valiantly to free itself from the ideas of identity and cause/effect that underlie classical science. Science, like the Tao (Way), urges us to get rid of all preconceived notions.

Whether the preconceived notion is that of the pre-Copernican universe or the assumption of cause and effect, conventional wisdom quickly grows obsolete, and it can bar the way to a deeper understanding. Elsewhere, Thich Nhat Hanh defines that understanding as "direct and immediate perception," "an intuition rather than the culmination of reasoning."

To cultivate direct, intuitive perception is the real work of the Zen practitioner. That work may be aided by the acquisition of conceptual knowledge, including intimate knowledge of Zen teachings and traditions. But unless that knowledge is integrated with direct experience, it can indeed become a positive hindrance. For the work of the Zen practitioner is to enter this present moment, becoming fully and sometimes fiercely aware of whatever is occurring. And as Roko Shinge Roshi has observed, to enter the present moment we "have to let go of everything extraneous—what we think regarding this moment, what we add to it, or try to take away from it." Practicing Zen is not a process of acquisition, nor is its aim the mastery of a body of knowledge. On the contrary, it is in large part a process of *un*learning, of becoming aware of our layers of conditioning rather than adding another layer.

To those of us who grew up in the competitive world of Western education, such a practice runs against the grain, and it may seem formidably foreign. But insofar as the aim of Zen practice is to help us navigate a complex, rapidly changing world, it shares common cause with our universities, colleges, and schools. And insofar as the practice engenders, as it often does, a passion for inquiry and a heightened

sense of discovery, its spirit is congruent with that of Western education. In each new moment, we are going back to
school.

September 2, 2010

The Sound of Tea

Of the sounds of this world, few are more pleasing than that of tea being poured, quietly and gently, into a porcelain cup.

That sound may he heard every Sunday evening, when the Falling Leaf Sangha, our local sitting group, meets to practice seated and walking meditation. With the striking of a gong, one of our members rises from her cushion. One by one, she serves us, pouring hot green tea into each of our cups. Amplified by the spacious, silent room, the trickling sound of tea brings to mind a bubbling stream or a miniature waterfall.

Listening to that sound in that place, I am sometimes reminded of the story of the monk Kyosho, who asked his teacher, Gensha (834–908), how to enter the practice of Zen.

"Do you hear the murmuring of the mountain stream?" asked Gensha.

"Yes," Kyosho replied.

"Then enter there."

With that reply, we are told, Kyosho experienced a spontaneous awakening.

To be sure, Gensha could have chosen other means. He could have advised his disciple to study Zen teachings and traditions. He could have prescribed a course of instruction. Instead, he exhorted Kyosho to *listen*: to put his logical, reasoning faculties in abeyance and to open his body and mind to the sounds of the world. In so doing, Gensha also pointed Kyosho toward an encounter with absolute reality and a deeper understanding of the self.

To listen with full attention to any sound is to awaken from one's daydreams and speculations and return to the reality of the here and now. In the story of Gensha and Kyosho, the sound could have been almost anything: the sough of wind in the trees, the scrape of sandals on the road, the sound of Kyosho's own name. By choosing water, however, Gensho called Kyosho's attention to a phenomenon that was unmistakably concrete, liquid, and transitory. As anyone who has listened to the flow of water knows, the sound induces a sense of calm, a mood of tranquility. But it also places the contemplative in the presence of impermanence, fostering the realization that what appears to be fixed is really fluid and subject to change. In time, the water in the mountain stream may become a lake, or ice, or a cloud, or water vapor. It is anything but solid.

And what is true of the stream is also true of all conditioned things, including the entity we are pleased to call the self. Zen teachings and the larger body of thought from which they derive do not propose that the self does not exist. Rather, they urge the recognition that what we imagine to be a solid self is in fact a fluid collection of experiences, a shifting aggregate of "form, feelings, perceptions, mental formations, and consciousness." And though we imagine that self to have an intrinsic existence, separate from the rest of the world, it is really an integral element in the web of life, susceptible like water to changing causes and conditions. The Zen teacher Charlotte Joko Beck likens it to a whirlpool in a river. Certainly that whirlpool exists, but it has no permanent form. We don't have to expend our energies pretending that it does, or attempting to hold it in place.

Paradoxically, the way to engender that liberating recognition is not to analyze the concept of emptiness, or struggle to envision the One Body of absolute reality, or engage in abstract thinking generally. Rather, it is to reconnect with what Zen calls our relative existence: our day-to-day, ordinary lives, experienced with openness and full awareness. And one of the best ways we can do this is through the act of listening, both to ourselves and to the world around us.

If you would like to demonstrate this to yourself, please sit still for a few minutes, following your breathing and collecting your scattered energies. Then do nothing but listen to whatever is occurring within and around you. If you are in a public space, listen to the voices in your environment, as they express their anxieties or joys, their elation or their sorrows. Listen, if you can, to what the novelist George Eliot called the "roar" on the "other side of silence"—the roar of human suffering. If you are at home, listen to your breathing, to the processes of your body, and to your ego as it arises, asserts itself in speech, and dissolves into the silence of awareness. Then, when you are ready, pour yourself a cup of tea, and listen to the sound.

September 16, 2010

The Leaves' Fossils

*I*f you have looked hard at a single object, you may have found that an image of the object lingers even after you've looked away.

Such is my experience every morning, when I drink green tea from a small porcelain cup. Looking down, I see the cup's white rim, which forms a perfect circle. Looking up, I see that same circle, now in black, projected against the bamboo rug. In its main features the image resembles the *enso*, or Zen circle—a symbol of enlightenment and absolute reality.

Not all images are so benign, nor is their duration so brief. The poet Ezra Pound famously defined the image as "an intellectual and emotional complex in an instant of time." And if that image is laden with emotional content, it may be virtually ineradicable. In her poem "Quai d' Orleans," Elizabeth Bishop observes barges on the river Seine, comparing their wakes to giant oak leaves, which extinguish themselves on the sides of the quay. Deepening her analogy, Bishop contrasts the disappearance of the wakes with the endurance of human memories, especially memories of loss. "If what we see could forget us half as easily," she reflects, "as it does itself—but for life we'll not be rid / of the leaves' fossils."

Zen meditation is essentially a process of stopping and looking. Amidst the multiple distractions of everyday life, the images in our psyches may well escape notice, but when we sit still, follow our breathing, and have a look at our interior lives, those images often return with a vengeance, bearing their cargo of memories and associations. How, if at all, should we respond to them? What, if anything, should we do?

Perhaps the most reflexive response is to pursue the image: to dwell in the past. Encountering the image of a barge, for example, I might recall the scenes of my childhood, when I sat for hours on the banks of the Mississippi River, watching the barges pass. Pushed by powerful "towboats," those massive platforms transported steel, coal, and other freight north toward Lock and Dam 13. Viewed from a distance, the barges appeared to be moving slowly, as they rounded the bend and gradually disappeared. But in fact they were moving at a rapid, dangerous clip, and boaters were well advised to stay out of their way. Remembering their bulk and speed, I recall that one of my schoolmates, a third grader named Michael Stone, drowned one night beneath a barge. A few days earlier, I had wrestled with him on the playground.

Such memories haunt us, and it is tempting to pursue them. But to do so is not the way of Zen meditation, whose aim is situate our minds and hearts, vividly and continuously, in the reality of the present moment. The *Bhaddekaratta Sutta* (*Sutra on the Better Way of Living Alone*), a guiding text for Zen practitioners, states this aim directly:

206

Do not pursue the past.
Do not lose yourself in the future.
The past no longer is.
The future has not yet come.
Looking deeply at life as it is
in the very here and now,
the practitioner dwells
in stability and freedom.

The sutra goes on to explain what is meant by "pursuing the past":

When someone thinks about the way his body was in the past, the way his feelings were in the past, the way his perceptions were in the past, the way his mental factors were in the past, the way his consciousness was in the past; when he thinks about these things and his mind is burdened by and attached to these things which belong to the past, then that person is pursuing the past.

By contrast, when a person thinks about those same things but his mind is neither "enslaved by nor attached" to them, then that person is not "pursuing the past."

To think about the past without being enslaved by it is a formidable challenge, but there are ways of meeting that challenge. Jack Kornfield, a clinical psychologist and renowned Vipassana teacher, advises us to heal the wounds in our psyches by bringing meditative awareness—"that which knows"—to our painful memories. Similarly, Zen master Thich Nhat Hanh urges us to review the past and "observe it deeply" while "standing firmly in the present." In that way our destructive memories can be transformed into something constructive. In either case, the method is first to ground ourselves in the present, and second, to cultivate a generous, clear awareness, in which images from the past, however troubling or enticing, arrive and last for a while but do not become objects of obsessive thought. Like barges observed from a river bank, they interest but do not overwhelm us.

September 30, 2010

What Were You Thinking?

One afternoon last summer, I did what many people seem to do: I stepped out of a hotel elevator and took a wrong turn. Realizing that I was headed toward a potted plant rather than my room, I did a discreet about-face, maintaining my dignity as best I could. "What were you thinking?" I asked myself. Assuming that I was thinking at all, my thoughts had not been in accord with reality.

To point the thinking mind in the direction of reality is an abiding aim of Zen meditation. In Zen teachings, such thought is called "Right Thinking," "right" meaning "in accordance with things as they are." To help us cultivate Right Thinking, Zen master Thich Nhat Hanh has devised four practices, which can be employed whenever we have a decision to make or a problem to solve. Taken singly, these practices help to align our thinking with reality. Taken together, they provide a guide to wise and harmonious living.

The first practice is to ask ourselves, "Are you sure?" As Thich Nhat Hanh has often observed, many of our perceptions are erroneous, and erroneous perceptions cause suffering. To take but one example, the recent Pew Forum survey of religious knowledge found that more than a quarter of Americans thought that the Golden Rule was one of the Ten Commandments. While that misperception is unlikely to cause much suffering, it well illustrates the disparity between belief and fact, a disparity that seems to be growing larger every day, as misinformation proliferates and is distributed at lightning speed. Thich Nhat Hanh recommends that we write "Are you sure?" on a large piece of paper and hang it where we will see it often. Perhaps it would make a good screen saver as well.

The second practice is to ask ourselves, "What am I doing?" Although the answer might seem obvious—"I am feeding the birds"; "I am reading a column on Zen meditation"—this question counters the habit of rushing into the future. It returns us to the present moment. For example, if you are up on a ladder cleaning out your gutters but thinking about something else, asking this question can bring your wandering mind back to the task at hand. That is important for your safety as well as your presence of mind. Asking "What am I doing?" can also reveal the extent to which our thoughts are conditioned—if not created—by whatever we are doing. Having that awareness, we may be less inclined to believe our passing thoughts or lose ourselves in speculation.

The third practice is to say, "Hello, habit energy." By "habit energies" Thich Nhat Hanh means our "ingrained thoughts," our habitual patterns of thinking and behaving. "Our way of acting depends on our way of thinking," he observes, "and our way of thinking depends on our habit energies." To become aware of those energies is often to diminish their power. And by addressing our habits directly, we accept and befriend them, rather than feel guilty about having them. Over time, this practice can keep us from applying tired, habitual ways of thinking to fresh situations. Insofar as we can recognize the habitual components in our thinking, we can respond with wisdom rather than react with reflexive judgment.

The fourth practice is *bodhicitta*, which translates as "the mind of love." In Thich Nhat Hanh's words, the mind of love is the "deep wish to cultivate understanding in ourselves in order to bring happiness to many beings." By making bodhicitta the basis of our thinking, we guide ourselves toward compassionate speech and action. This practice may well be the most important of the four, but in my experience it is also the one most likely to be forgotten when conflict arises. How easy it is to think poorly of someone who has insulted us. How hard it is to cultivate the mind of love when subjected to calumny or manifest injustice. Yet not to do so is to cloud one's thinking and to foster speech and actions that one may later regret. Like the other practices, bodhicitta affords us protection as well as guidance, steering us away from actions that will do harm to ourselves and others.

As Thich Nhat Hanh makes clear, the practice of Right Thinking is not a substitute for meditation. The practice is merely a "map," and when we have arrived at our destination, "we need to put down the map and enter the reality fully." That is sound advice, especially for the practice of Zen, which regards conceptual thinking, however wise or foolish, as a barrier to the direct experience of reality. But the map provided by Thich Nhat Hanh can prepare us for meditation, and it can assist us in implementing meditative insight. Like a patient friend, it can help us find our way.

October 14, 2010

Hope Is Not a Plan

*I*n "Letting Go," an illuminating article on care for the dying, the surgeon and author Atul Gawande examines the choices that terminal patients and their families face at the end of life. Contrasting hospice with hospital care, he reports a remarkable finding:

> *Like many people, I had believed that hospice care hastens death, because patients forgo hospital treatments and are allowed high-dose narcotics to combat pain. But studies suggest otherwise. In one, researchers followed 4,493 Medicare patients with either terminal cancer or congestive heart failure. They found no difference in survival time between hospice and non-hospice patients with breast cancer, prostate cancer, and colon cancer. Curiously, hospice care seemed to extend survival for some patients; those with pancreatic cancer gained an average of three weeks, those with lung cancer gained six weeks, and those with congestive heart failure gained three months.*

Reflecting on this finding, Dr. Gawande concludes that the "lesson seems almost Zen: you live longer only when you stop trying to live longer."

"Almost Zen" is an approximation, akin to the modifier "Zen-like," which often obscures what it purports to describe. But in associating this particular "lesson" with Zen practice, Dr. Gawande comes close to the mark. Shunryu Suzuki Roshi, author of *Zen Mind, Beginner's Mind*, often admonished his students to have "no gaining idea" when practicing Zen meditation. Other teachers have done the same. Those Medicare patients who chose to forgo hospital treatment were indeed rejecting a gaining idea: that of a longer life at any cost. Ironically, by choosing hospice care, they not only improved the quality of their last days and avoided the debilitating side-effects of hospital treatments. They also lengthened their lives.

Yet it is one thing to know that you have a fatal illness and another to accept that you are dying. "I'd say only a quarter have accepted their fate when they come into hospice," observes Sarah Creed, a hospice nurse quoted by Dr. Gawande. "Ninety-nine per cent understand that they are dying, but one hundred per cent hope they're not. They still want to beat their disease." Such hope is only human. Only a very cold observer would presume to judge it adversely. But to deny that one is dying, when that is in fact the case, is not a constructive way to prepare oneself or one's loved ones for the inevitable. Nor is it the way of Zen.

The Zen teacher Charlotte Joko Beck, who is nothing if not tough-minded, once proclaimed that to practice Zen, we have to "give up hope." When that statement angered some of her students, she explained what she had meant:

Sounds terrible, doesn't it? Actually, it's not terrible at all. A life lived with no hope is a peaceful, joyous, compassionate life. ... [W]e are usually living in vain hope for something or someone that will make my life easier, more pleasant. We spend most of our time trying to set life up in a way so that will be true; when, contrariwise, the joy of our life is just in totally doing and bearing what must be borne, in just doing what has to be done. It's not even what has to be done; it's there to be done so we do it.

Joko Beck's tone is blunt, and her perspective may be difficult to accept. But that perspective accords with Dr. Gawande's, insofar as it admonishes us to accept the harshest of realities and to act accordingly. Addressing the question of hope, Dr. Gawande recalls the example of Stephen Jay Gould, who survived a rare and lethal cancer for twenty years. "I think of Gould," Dr. Gawande remarks, "every time I have a patient with terminal illness. There is almost always a long tail of possibility, however thin." There is nothing wrong with looking for that tail, he acknowledges, "unless it means we have failed to prepare for the outcome that's vastly more probable." What is wrong is that "we have created a multitrillion-dollar edifice for dispensing the medical equivalent of lottery tickets ... Hope is not a plan, but hope is our plan." As a wiser alternative, he advocates open discussions, funded by medical insurance, between terminal patients, their families, and their doctors. Conducted with patience and candor, discussions of this kind can clarify what is most important to the dying person. And having had such discussions, people are "far more likely to die at peace and in control of their situation, and to spare their family anguish."

Reading Dr. Gawande's prescription, I am reminded of the experience of Shinge Roko Sherry Chayat Roshi, Abbot of the Zen Center of Syracuse, whose mother recently passed away. During the days before her death, Shinge Roshi talked with her mother about books, art, and music. She edited her mother's memoirs—and helped her write the ending. Her mother, in turn, saw to it that her affairs were in order. Accepting her imminent death, she gave her daughter a list of things to do, people to call, and last thoughts. For Shinge Roshi, the experience of being with her mother during and after her passing awakened feelings of profound gratitude. It was, she said, as miraculous as birth.

October 28, 2010

Children from the Sun

"Calm the heart's dark waters," advised the third-century Chinese poet Lu Chi. "Collect from deep thoughts the proper names for things."

I was reminded of Lu Chi's admonition the other day, when I came upon a poem by the Irish poet Pearse Hutchinson (b. 1927). Entitled "She Fell Asleep in the Sun," the poem concerns the children of unwed mothers. Embedding Irish-Gaelic phrases within his English text, Hutchinson presents two, very different ways of describing such children. In so doing, he also presents two contrasting perspectives on human frailty.

"She fell asleep in the sun," explains the narrator of the poem, is an Irish way of saying that a young woman got pregnant unintentionally. "That's what they used to say," the narrator recalls, "in South Fermanagh / of a girl who gave birth / unwed." Shifting the scene to County Kerry, the narrator invokes a phrase used in that part of the country: *"leanbh ón ngréin:* / a child from the sun." As a third example, he describes another "child from the sun": a "little lad running round a farmyard" in North Tipperary. Watching the child, his "granda" remarks that the boy is *"garsúinín beag mishtake."* That phrase may be translated as "the little lad's a mistake" or "the lad's a little mistake."

Taken together, the Irish phrases in Hutchinson's poem express an attitude of realism, acceptance, and forgiveness. In subsequent stanzas, the narrator praises that attitude—and wonders whether it can survive in modern times:

> *A lyrical ancient kindness*
> *that could with Christ accord.*
> *Can it outlive technolatry?*
> *or churches?*

> *Not to mention that long, leadránach,*
> *latinate, legal, ugly*
> *twelve-letter name not*
> *worthy to be called a name,*
> *that murderous obscenity—to call*

> *any child ever born*
> *that excuse for a name*
> *could quench the sun for ever.*

Pairing a narrow morality, as preached in certain churches, with the worship of technology, these lines inquire whether the Christ-like kindness of the older culture can endure in twentieth-century Ireland. Embodied in the phrases of an endangered language, that kindness seems itself endangered, a mode of feeling that may soon be leaving the world.

Among the forces eroding that mode of feeling, Hutchinson cites a "legal, ugly / twelve-letter name." As the reader may readily infer, that unspoken, Latinate name is *illegitimate*. In contrast to the vivid, concrete Irish phrases, the abstract English word conveys a tedious (*leadránach*), judgmental attitude toward the mother's "mistake" and the child who must bear the consequences of her actions. Rather than welcome the child into the human family, the English word defines him as an outcast, murdering his spirit and quenching the life-giving sun.

Of the two perspectives in his poem, Hutchinson clearly favors the first. Adopting that perspective, we might empathize with the plight of mother and child. We might look into the conditions that brought her son into being and try to imagine the life ahead of him. And we might also admit that at times we have done foolish, irresponsible things ourselves. Adopting the second perspective, however, we might observe that the child is indeed illegitimate, as judged by accepted norms, and that to call him a *child from the sun* is to soften a social reality, poeticize a legal fact, and implicitly condone unwed motherhood. In passing we might note that calling a child a "mistake" may be only a little less damaging than calling him illegitimate.

One of the virtues of meditative practice, Zen included, is that it allows us the space and freedom to examine our responses to human frailty, whether judgmental or compassionate or somewhere in between, before taking action or saying a word. In contemporary American culture, the judgmental response has become reflexive, even in putatively "spiritual" circles. But a compassionate response is also possible, and the mind of compassion is often more penetrating than that of moral judgment, which tends to distance us from the conditions of human suffering. And should we deign to look deeply into the heart's dark waters, we may discover that in our own ways we too are children from the sun.

November 11, 2010

The Life I Have Been Given

O ver the past year we have heard a great deal about collective anger. During the run-up to the mid-term elections, the news media provided daily reports on the anger of the American electorate, and it would appear that many took their anger to the polls. However, amidst all the expressions of anger, political and otherwise, words of gratitude have been in short supply. Now that the season of thanksgiving is upon us, where shall we find those words?

The world's great spiritual traditions abound in expressions of gratitude, and if you are affiliated with one of those traditions, you may already have all the words you need. If you are not, however, or if you would like to refresh your sense of gratitude, you may wish to explore three practices from the Zen and Vipassana traditions.

The first practice concerns the body, which many of us take for granted. If our organs and limbs are functioning normally and causing us no discomfort, we often give them scant attention, sometimes at the expense of our well-being.

To counter that tendency, Zen master Thich Nhat Hanh rec-ommends that we sit still, follow our breathing, and silently recite verses such as these:

Breathing in, I know that I have two good eyes
Breathing out, I feel joy

- - -

Breathing in, I am aware of my heart
Breathing out, I am grateful for my heart

Proceeding through the various parts of our bodies, as a doctor might, we acknowledge the normal functioning of our lungs, stomach, liver, and so on. We express our grati-tude that each is serving us well. The purpose of this exercise is not to cheer ourselves up or convince ourselves that we feel something we don't. Rather, it is to put us in touch with our latent capacity for gratitude, which may have yet to manifest in conscious feeling. In Vipassana meditation, such practices are known as *bhavana*, or mind/body cultivation, and they are an essential component of meditative discipline.

A second practice is the meal chant. Comparable to grace-before-meals in the Judeo-Christian tradition, this practice raises our awareness of the nature and origin of the food we are about to eat. Here is Thich Nhat Hanh's translation of one traditional text, known in Zen as the Five Contemplations:

This food is the gift of the whole universe: the earth, the
*   sky, and much hard work.*

May we live in mindfulness so as to be worthy to receive it.

May we transform our unskillful states of mind and
*   learn to eat with moderation.*
May we take only foods that nourish us and prevent illness.

*We accept this food so that we may realize the path of
understanding and love.*

In Zen centers and monasteries around the world, these
lines and others like them are chanted or recited in unison
before each of the daily meals. For secular Westerners, group
recitation may be impractical, but anyone can silently recite
the Five Contemplations before tucking into a meal, whether
the food on the table be a red-lentil curry or turkey with all
the trimmings. Practiced wholeheartedly, meal chants can
change our relationship, gradually but radically, with the
food we consume.

The third practice is the most general of the three. For-
mulated by the Vipassana teacher Jack Kornfield, it is a kind
of litany, which expresses gratitude not only for our bodies
and our food but for our very presence in the cosmos:

*With gratitude I remember the people, animals, plants,
insects, creatures of the sky and sea, air and water,
fire and earth, all whose joyful exertion blesses my
life every day.*

*With gratitude I remember the care and labor of a thou-
sand generations of elders and ancestors who came
before me.*

*I offer my gratitude for the safety and well-being I have
been given.*

*I offer my gratitude for the blessings of this earth I have
been given.*

*I offer my gratitude for the measure of health I have been
given.*

*I offer my gratitude for the family and friends I have been
    given.*

I offer my gratitude for the community I have been given.

*I offer my gratitude for the teachings and lessons I have
    been given.*

I offer my gratitude for the life I have been given.

Although this text is particularly apt for the Thanksgiving holiday, it really knows no season. It can be recited, singly or collectively, at any time or place, and its cumulative effect can be transformative.

The late John Daido Loori Roshi once remarked that if we voiced our gratitude rather than our complaints every morning, in a year's time we would become grateful people. That is a lot to ask, especially when anger is so pervasive, and when there is so much to fear and complain about. But as a succinct reminder, here is a poem by the twelfth-century Japanese poet Saigyo:

GRATITUDE

Whatever it is,
I cannot understand it,
although gratitude
stubbornly overcomes me
until I'm reduced to tears.

If this poem speaks to you, you might post it on your fridge. Or perhaps above your TV.

November 25, 2010

Habits of Mind

"*El* Noi de la Mare" ("The Son of Mary") is a traditional Catalonian folksong. Originally a Christmas carol, this anonymous, sixteenth-century melody was arranged for guitar by Miguel Llobet (1878–1938) and brought to prominence by the great twentieth-century guitarist Andres Segovia. Since then, generations of classical guitarists have played it as an encore.

I first heard "El Noi de la Mare" some thirty years ago. Recently, I chanced to hear it again and decided to add it to my repertoire. After working out the technical problems of the piece (its simple, arch-shaped phrases belie complex fingerings and challenging position-changes), I recorded it, hoping to gain some insight. To my chagrin, I discovered that I had unintentionally arpeggiated many chords, which is to say, I had broken them into successions of notes. I was reminded of a comment by the concert guitarist Alice Artzt, for whom I once played a movement from Bach's first cello suite. "You have Segovia's disease," she wryly noted, having listened to me break chords that should never have been broken.

224

To arpeggiate a chord is not in itself a technical flaw. Properly executed and appropriately placed, arpeggios can impart a harp-like feeling to a phrase or cadence. Played on the guitar, arpeggios may also add a dreamy Spanish flavor, evoking afternoons in Madrid or nights in Barcelona. Andres Segovia made frequent use of arpeggios, even in the Baroque music he transcribed for guitar, and at times they seemed strangely at odds with the music he was playing. In my youth I listened avidly to Segovia. And as I learned in recording "El Noi de la Mare," I have carried his manner with me to this day.

In his memoir *Practicing: A Musician's Return to Music*, the classical guitarist Glenn Kurtz describes musical performance as a "battleground between your habits and your ideal." Recalling his struggle to play a study by Fernando Sor, he elaborates the point:

> *Technique, like the body's memory, is gloriously reliable and stubbornly resistant to change. Try to alter the way you hold a fork, or the way you face your spouse when angry. If you really concentrate, then it isn't hard to do. But the moment you are distracted—the moment you begin to rely on your habits, your technique—you slip back into established patterns. Fixing mistakes is easy. Correcting your technique means undoing all your previous practice. You have to replace one habit with another, better one.*

And just as specific habits must be addressed, so must one's habitual attitude toward one's instrument. In Kurtz's words, "it's not just this one passage, this one movement that I need to change, but a whole lifetime of movement, my whole history."

Digital recording provides an immediate, accurate, and unforgiving means by which a musician can become aware of unconscious habits. And the same might be said of Zen meditation, which brings real-time awareness to our habitual responses. *Habits of mind*, we sometimes call them, but they are also habits of feeling, perception, and moral judgment. The way we face our spouse (or partner or parent or child) may well be habitual, and so may the cast of mind we bring to that encounter. What the satirist Jonathan Swift called the prejudices of our education and Zen calls our conditioning often determines what we see and how we see it. And rather than erode, our mental ruts tend to deepen as we grow older.

Yet it is possible to "take the backward step that illuminates the self," as the thirteenth-century Zen master Eihei Dogen advised us to do, and to become aware of our mental habits even as they are arising. Should we do that, we may find that we are firmly attached to our habitual responses. As the meditation teacher Pema Chodron puts it, we wear them like clothes, and we don't want to take them off, lest we be "too exposed, naked in front of everyone." Through diligent attention, however, we can weaken the hold of habits in our lives. We can come to see them clearly. And over time, we may also learn how to drop them, clearing the way for a fresh response.

According to one report, the sheet music for "El Noi de la Mare" was open on Andres Segovia's music stand on the day he died. It may well have been the last piece he played. What better tribute to his memory—and to the music itself—than to play the piece with as much freshness as one can muster, adding arpeggios only when indicated or when the music itself invites them? And what better way to honor our everyday experience than to respond as openly as we can manage, unimpeded by our longstanding habits of mind?

December 16, 2010

Leaning into the Curves

*T*oward the end of Richard Russo's novel *Bridge of Sighs,* a middle-aged widow named Tessa Lynch recalls a wild ride on the back of a motorcycle. A teenager at the time, Tessa defied her parents by secretly consorting with Declan, a reckless, dangerous man, recently discharged from the army, who rode an Indian motorcycle. When Declan invited Tessa to ride with him, she eagerly accepted. And when he opened the throttle she showed no fear. In Declan's eyes she was "a natural the way she rode … leaning into the curves instead of away, as you would if you were afraid."

In Russo's novel, the act of leaning into the curves becomes a metaphor for a bold and open attitude toward life. In similar fashion, the meditation teacher Pema Chodron employs the metaphor of leaning-in to illustrate a way of dealing with fear, anger, and other destructive states of mind. Enlisting the Tibetan concept of *shenpa*, which she translates as "hooked," Chodron advocates a three-step method, the first step being acknowledgment that one has been "hooked" by negative feeling. The second step is to "lean into" that feeling:

> Step Two. Pause, take three conscious breaths, and lean in. Lean in to the energy. Abide with it. Experience it fully. Taste it. Touch it. Smell it. Get curious about it. How does it feel in your body? What thoughts does it give birth to? Become very intimate with the itch and urge of shenpa and keep breathing. Part of this step is learning not to be seduced by the momentum of shenpa. Like Ulysses, we can find our way to hear the call of the sirens without being seduced. It's a process of staying awake and compassionate, interrupting the momentum, and refraining from causing harm. Just do not speak, do not act, and feel the energy. Be one with your own energy, one with the ebb and flow of life. Rather than rejecting the energy, embrace it. This leaning in is very open, very curious and intelligent.

Having learned to "lean in," to "embrace the restless energy," we can proceed to the third step, which is to "relax and move on."

As Chodron readily acknowledges, leaning into uncomfortable emotions is far from easy. It takes awareness, and it also takes practice. If, for example, someone unjustly accuses us, our habitual response may be to counterattack—or flee the scene entirely. Rather than remain "awake and compassionate," we are more likely to blame the accuser and retreat into a "storyline," in which we appear as virtuous victims and others as vicious tormentors. And what we resist or attempt to elude is not only the object of our fear or anger; it is also those emotional states themselves. Rather than encounter and attempt to transform their negative energies, we escape into self-exonerating fantasies. Hooked on *shenpa*, we inflict suffering on ourselves and others, while also putting distance between our abstract thoughts and our ever-changing feelings. We lean away from the reality of our lives.

Yet it is possible to do otherwise. Merely by stopping, checking in with ourselves, and bringing awareness to our mental states, we can begin to "unhook" ourselves from destructive, habitual responses. And over time the practice of mindfulness can also incline our minds toward direct contact with our inner and external lives. Reflecting on recent studies of Mindfulness-Based Stress Reduction, Dr. Daniel Siegel, a physician and meditative practitioner, offers this perspective:

> One of the elements of research on Mindfulness-Based Stress Reduction that I find most impressive is the work that Richie Davidson and Jon [Kabat-Zinn] have done showing that even after one eight-week MBSR course, a "left-shift" has been noted, in which the left frontal activity of the brain is enhanced. This electrical change in brain function is thought to reflect the cultivation of an "approach state," in which we move toward, rather than away from, a challenging external situation or internal mental function such as a thought, feeling, or memory. Such an approach can be seen as the neural basis for resilience. With a mindful way of being, you've developed your skill to stay present for what you might otherwise try to escape. From that point of view, diagnosis would be enhanced, because denial would be overcome. If you think about it, this is the mind doing what is most helpful for mind and body. Ignoring is maladaptive.

Paradoxically, it takes courage to face one's fear. For many of us, the "approach state" does not come naturally, and leaning into the curves is an acquired skill. But the New Year has arrived, and a resolution to lean into our experience, however pleasant or unpleasant, delectable or undesirable, is well worth considering. As New Year's resolutions go, it is difficult to think of one more capable of transforming fear into fearlessness, anger into compassion, and habitual denial into wisdom.

January 13, 2011

Effortless Effort

*E*very morning at half-past six, I make a cup of coffee for my wife, using a device known as an AeroPress. Simplicity itself, this device consists of a plunger, a cylinder, a paper filter, and a perforated cap. To brew a cup of coffee, I place the AeroPress on top of a mug, pour the prescribed amount of freshly ground coffee into the cylinder, and add a small amount of hot water to release the flavor. Moments later, I add the full complement of hot water, insert the plunger, and press down. If I press too hard, I will encounter formidable resistance from the volume of air trapped between the plunger and the coffee, and the AeroPress won't work. But if I press gently, with virtually no effort, the plunger will go down smoothly, emitting an audible sigh as it reaches the bottom. Almost always, the result will be a delicious cup of coffee.

I first heard about the AeroPress from a friend and fellow Zen practitioner, who also makes morning coffee for his missus. That is perhaps no accident, because the skills required to operate the AeroPress resemble their counterparts in Zen meditation. Both the AeroPress and the practice of Zen require balance, patience, and steady attention. Beyond that, both enlist the kind of energy known to Taoists as *wu wei*, or "effortless effort," whether the object of the effort be the breath, the contents of the mind, or the situations encountered in everyday life. Press too hard, and you will fail. Press lightly, aligning yourself with natural forces, and you will allow the desired result to occur.

Most meditative practices begin with attention to the breath. Some schools of meditation, including Zen, advocate the counting of breaths in general and exhalations in particular. Others employ such words as "in" and "out" to track the process of respiration. Whatever the method, however, many people find it difficult to observe the process of breathing without attempting to control that process or bring it into conformity with an imagined ideal. To counter that tendency, I have found it helpful merely to *listen* to the breath, as the Zen-trained teacher Toni Packer advises, rather than employ an analytic method. In the same spirit, one can view oneself not as the owner/operator of one's breathing but as the one "being breathed," both by one's body and by the life force common to all living beings. Approached in this way, the breath becomes an object of interest rather than willful concentration.

Turning from the breath to the contents of the mind, the same quality of attention may be applied. In his essay "Samadhi of the Self," the Soto master Menzan Zenji (1683–1769) defines the contents of the mind as "emotion-thought," which he views as "the root of delusion; that is, a stubborn attachment to a one-sided point of view, formed

233

by our own conditioned perceptions." The purpose of *zazen*, or sitting meditation, is not to suppress thoughts, as some would have it, but to clarify "how emotion-thought melts." Through the regular practice of zazen, "the frozen block of emotion-thought will naturally melt away." This will occur not through cutting off thought, a practice Menzan likens to cutting the trunk of a tree and leaving the root alive. Rather, it will occur through effortless effort: through mindful observation of self-centered thoughts and their emotional subtexts. The equivalent of a gentle hand on the AeroPress, such observation serves to illuminate the roots, the dynamics, and the consequences of ego-centered, prejudicial thinking. Over time, it can thaw the frozen block of emotion-thought.

But can that degree of awareness, attainable within the confines of private meditation, be sustained within the arena of everyday life? Can it withstand the violence, physical and verbal, of contemporary culture? In his address in Tucson on January 12, President Obama invited us to ask ourselves whether "we've shown enough kindness and generosity and compassion to the people in our lives." He also asserted that "what matters is not wealth, or status, or power, or fame" but "how well we may have loved." Those are stirring words, and they rightly locate the nexus of non-violence in immediate, human interaction. At the same time, they remind us of the centuries of negative conditioning—the monumental blocks of emotion-thought—that must be addressed with awareness, if the President's vision of a kinder society is to be realized.

Given present conditions, that may seem a Herculean project, requiring nothing short of a social and spiritual revolution. But such a project can begin with an effortless effort, which is to say, with a clear and intimate awareness of what we are about to say or do in this very moment. Living in that awareness, we can ask ourselves whether what we're about to say is necessary, true, and kind, and whether our words and actions are likely to be hurtful or harmful. And we can speak and act accordingly.

January 27, 2011

NOTES

Ichigo Ichie

5 **In 1860 Naosuke**: Eido Tai Shimano and Kogetsu Tani, *Zen Word, Zen Calligraphy* (Shambhala, 1995), 35.

We are always at the beginning: Maurine Stuart, *Subtle Sound* (Shambhala, 1996), 16.

Zenlike Peace

10 **Sitting in the makeup chair**: Michael Crowley, "Hillary's Non-muskie Moment," *The Stump*, January 7, 2008. http://www.tnr.com/blog/the-stump/hillarys-non-muskie-moment.

11 **To think that people**: Kosho Uchiyama, *Opening the Hand of Thought* (Wisdom, 2004), 18-19.

When we let go of our conceptions: Uchiyama, 12.

Habit Energies

16 **Even in the middle of the night**: W.S. Merwin, *Writings to an Unfinished Accompaniment* (Atheneum, 1973), 28.

Of Fountain Pens and Emptiness

20 **Once you realize**: Eckhart Tolle, *A New Earth* (Penguin, 2005), 81.

Sitting without Goals

23 **What is there before**: *Opening the Hand of Thought*, 30.

Just This

26 **If the first trains us**: James H. Austin, *Zen-Brain Reflections* (MIT Press, 2006), 33-37.

Zen and the Classifieds

30 **In his new book**: Jack Kornfield, *The Wise Heart* (Bantam, 2008), 42.

Cooking with Dogen

38 **The affinity between cooking and Zen:** *Moon in a Dewdrop: Writings of Zen Master Dogen*, ed. Kazuaki Tanahashi (North Point Press, 1985), 53-66.

Springwater

41 **There are different states of mind:** Toni Packer, *The Work of This Moment* (Tuttle, 1995), 1,4.

42 **Can there be listening:** Packer, 4.

Innocence

43 **And in "Stony Grey Soil":** Patrick Kavanagh, *The Complete Poems* (Peter Kavanagh Hand Press, 1972), 73.

44 **They laughed at one I loved:** *The Complete Poems*, 241.

45 **The goal of practice:** Shunryu Suzuki, *Zen Mind, Beginner's Mind* (Weatherhill, 1970), 21.

Firewood and Ashes

46 **Firewood becomes ashes:** Eihei Dogen, "Actualizing the Fundamental Point" (*Genjo Koan*), tr. by Yasuda Joshu Roshi and Anzan Hoshin Roshi, *Dogen: Zen Writings on the Practice of Realization*, forthcoming. See http://www.wwzc.org/node/279.

47 **Zen Master Dogen once said:** Toni Packer, "Firewood Does Not Turn into Ashes," *Springwater Center Newsletter*, Summer, 2003, 1-2.

Stability and Resilience

49 **At its current height:** Since this column was written, the Burj Dubai has been renamed the Burj Khalifa. For my understanding of stability and resilience I am indebted to Will Johnson's *The Posture of Meditation* (Shambhala, 1996).

Just Sitting

62 **This is zazen:** *Namu Dai Bosa*, ed. Louis Nordstrom (Theatre Arts Books, 1976), 251.

The Tow Rope

64 **Neglectful, we've yet:** *Saigyo: Poems of a Mountain Home*, tr. Burton Watson (Columbia University Press, 1991), 94.

108 Delusions

71 **We say 108:** Anzan Hoshin Roshi, "Joya: Resolutions," http://www.wwzc.org/teisho/joya.htm.

We desire permanent existence: Robert Aitken, *The Dragon Who Never Sleeps* (Parallax, 1992), xiii.

Ice Dams

73 **Water is soft and fluid:** *Shambhala Sun* (January, 2009), 78-79.

Not-Knowing

76 **In the blue night:** Gary Snyder, *Turtle Island* (New Directions, 1974). To hear Gary Snyder read "Pine Tree Tops," go to http://cdn3.libsyn.com/bubba/Gary_Snyder_Spiritual_Spice_14.mp3?nvb=20091124134834&nva=200911251.

Preferences

79 **The Great Way is not difficult:** Seng-ts'an, *Verses on the Faith-Mind*, tr. Richard B. Clarke, http://www.mendosa.com/way.html.

80 **Sometimes people say:** Toni Packer, *The Wonder of Presence* (Shambhala, 2002), 134.

As Surely as One's Shadow

86 **Mind is the forerunner of action:** *The Dhammapada*, tr. Ven. Ananda Maitreya (Parallax Press 1995), 1.

The Mother Road

89 **If we observe these materials deeply:** Thich Nhat Hanh, *Our Appointment with Life* (Parallax, 1990), 33.

The full text of John Casesa's remarks may be found at http://www.onearth.org/article/motown-blues.

Flint's Auto Center is located at 63 Main Street in Almond, New York.

A Single Gentian

91 **At Poll Salach**: "At Poll Salach" appears in Michael Longley's collection *The Weather in Japan* (Wake Forest University Press, 2000). It is reprinted here by permission of Wake Forest University Press.

The Thoughtless People

96 **In any given moment:** Jon Kabat-Zinn, *Coming to Our Senses* (Hyperion, 2005), 71.

A Sense of Ceremony

99 **The making of a bed:** Brother Joseph Keenan, "Tea for All Nations: The Japanese Tea Ceremony": http://web.archive.org/web/20080528100807/www.teahyakka.com/keenanlayout.html.

Stepping Stones

103 **Suddenly you were on your own:** Seamus Heaney, *Finders Keepers* (Faber, 2002), 48.

Seven Words

106 **That experience:** *Atlantic Unbound*, September, 1997.

108 **Zazen is both something one *does*:** Eido Tai Shimano Roshi, "What is Zen," http://www.amacord.com/taste/essays/zen.html.

Me and Mu

110 **And millions of the rest of us**: Philip Booth, *Selves* (Viking, 1990), 56.

111 **In our ordinary discriminatory world:** Thich Nhat Hanh, *Transformation at the Base: Fifty Verses on the Nature of Consciousness* (Parallax Press, 2001), 77.

Resting

118 **During our sitting meditation:** Thich Nhat Hanh, "Resting in the River," http://www.pathandfruit.com/Books2/Thich_Nhat_Hanh_Resting_in_the_River.html.

119 **I wish to bear in mind:** *A Conservationist Manifesto* (Indiana University Press, 2009), 199.

Taking Care

124 **In Zen kitchens:** Stephanie Kaza, *Mindfully Green: A Personal and Spiritual Guide to Whole Earth Thinking* (Shambhala, 2008), 135.

125 **To meditate means to go home:** Thich Nhat Hanh, "This Is the Buddha's Love," an interview with Melvin McLeod, *Shambhala Sun* (2008), http://www.shambhalasun.com/index.php?option=content&task=view&id=2882.

A Mighty Wave

131 **"I turned toward the disease":** Quoted in *Buddhadharma* (Fall 2009), 47.

Closing Doors

133 **The master can see:** Thich Nhat Hanh, *Zen Keys* (Thorsons, 1995), 29.

134 **Men at forty:** Donald Justice, *New and Selected Poems* (Knopf, 1995), 76.

Transitions are like doorways: Judith L. Lief, *Making Friends with Death* (Shambhala, 2001), 15.

The Tempo of Meditation

141 **Hurrying is antithetical:** Arthur Zajonc, *Meditation as Contemplative Inquiry* (Lindisfarne, 2009), 98.

Weathered Wood

143 **Sabi by itself means "the bloom of time":** Tadao Ando, "What is Wabi-Sabi?" http://nobleharbor.com/tea/chado/WhatIsWabi-Sabi.htm.

144 **The *furyu* [*sabi*] of this bamboo:** Daisetz T. Suzuki, *Zen and Japanese Culture* (Princeton, 1970), 326.

See also Leonard Koren, *Wabi-Sabi for Artists, Designers, Poets, & Philosophers* (Berkeley: Stone Bridge Press, 1994).

Silence and Intimacy

146 **Only when I am quiet:** Jane Hirshfield, "Only When I Am Quiet and Do Not Speak," *Given Sugar, Given Salt* (HarperCollins, 2001), 23.

"I'm never free of fear": Toni Packer, *The Wonder of Presence* (Shambhala, 2002), 59.

147 **All of us can watch *me*-ness:** *The Wonder of Presence*, 82.

The family of things: Mary Oliver, "Wild Geese," *Dream Work* (Atlantic Monthly Press, 1986), 14.

Looking Deeply

154 **Writing is a practice:** Thich Nhat Hanh, *The Heart of the Buddha's Teaching* (Parallax, 1998), 83.

155 **They could not keep me from wells:** "Personal Helicon," Seamus Heaney, *Opened Ground* (Farrar, Straus, and Giroux, 1998), 14.

A Fundamental Perplexity

157 **The ultimate aim of Zen:** Roshi Philip Kapleau, *Zen: Merging of East and West* (Anchor, 1979), 132.

The active, powerful, fundamental: Zoketsu Norman Fischer, "On Questioning," *Mountains are Mountains and Rivers are Rivers*, ed. Ilana Rabinowitz (Hyperion, 1999), 17.

Dappled Things

160 **Glory be to God:** Gerard Manley Hopkins, "Pied Beauty," *The Major Works* (Oxford, 2002), 132.

It is due to our grasping and rejecting: Seng-ts'an, *Verses on the Faith-Mind*, tr. Richard B. Clarke. See http://www.mendosa.com/way.html.

161 **A fishy smell**: *The Essential Haiku,* ed. Robert Hass (Ecco, 1994), 35, 39.

Eight-petaled yellow "Shell" sign: Gary Snyder, "In the Santa Clarita Valley," *Danger on Peaks* (Shoemaker and Hoard, 2004), 67.

Carols, Hymns, and Chants

163 **The folk-song of religious music:** Sir Henry Hadow, "Carol Singing," *Times Literary Supplement,* January 2, 1903.

165 **Zen chanting grounds the practitioner**: John Daido Loori Roshi, *Bringing the Sacred to Life: The Daily Practice of Zen Ritual* (Shambhala, 2008), 65-66.

Leaving Things Alone

169 **"Zazen," writes the Soto master**: Kosho Uchiyama, *Opening the Hand of Thought* (Wisdom, 2004), 102.

170 **Squeeze it lightly**: Omori Sogen, *An Introduction to Zen Training* (Tuttle, 2001), 42.

Holding the diaphragm: Katsuki Sekida, *Zen Training* (Weatherhill, 1985), 56.

Drop everything: *Opening the Hand of Thought,* 48.

171 **No need to be rigid:** Toni Packer, *The Wonder of Presence* (Shambhala, 2002), 17.

"Gaze at the world but leave the world alone" is the Irish poet Derek Mahon's paraphrase of Chuang Tzu's admonition:

> *We have lost our equilibrium, he said;*
> *gaze at the world but leave the world alone.*
> *Do nothing; do nothing and everything will be done.*
>
> —Derek Mahon, *The Yellow Book*
> (Wake Forest University Press, 1998), 50

The Sword of Attention

173 **Our original mind:** Shunryu Suzuki Roshi, *Zen Mind, Beginner's Mind* (Weatherhill, 1970), 21.

A zendo is not a place: Charlotte Joko Beck, *Everyday Zen* (HarperCollins, 1989), 32.

From Rouge to the Color of Moonlight

179 **In the world of these phenomena:** Miyazawa Kenji, "Past Desire," *Selections,* ed. Hiroaki Sato (University of California Press, 2007), 100.

180 **A mind that is free:** Mu Soeng, ed., *The Diamond Sutra* (Wisdom, 2000), 110.

That mind that is not caught up: Thich Nhat Hanh, *The Diamond that Cuts through Illusion* (Parallax, 1992), 78.

Batter Up

181 **I've conceded the fact:** Bryan Hoch, "A-Rod Belts Historic Homer," *yankees.com,* August 4, 2007.

182 **And very suddenly:** Peter Matthiessen, *Nine-Headed Dragon River: Zen Journals* (Shambhala, 1998), 129-130.

To think that people: Kosho Uchiyama, *Opening the Hand of Thought* (Wisdom, 2004), 18-19.

183 **Although the novice:** T.P. Kasulis, *Zen Action, Zen Person* (University Press of Hawaii, 1981), 58.

I think kensho is essential: Matthiessen,126.

Saying Nothing

184 **Holiness is only the word:** Thich Nhat Hanh, *Nothing to Do, Nowhere to Go* (Parallax, 2007), 122.

186 **A mosquito's estimation of her meal:** Jane Hirshfield, *After* (HarperCollins, 2006), 41.

No writing on the solitary: Thomas Merton, *Echoing Silence,* ed. Robert Inchausti (New Seeds, 2007), 55.

Here and There

189 **In ordinary thinking:** Charlotte Joko Beck, *Nothing Special: Living Zen* (HarperSanFrancisco, 1993), 152.

Closing the Gap

193 **We have to dissolve all prejudices:** Thich Nhat Hanh, *Living Buddha, Living Christ* (Riverhead, 1995), 101.

Deep listening and loving speech: Thich Nhat Hanh, *Creating True Peace* (Free Press, 2003), 88.

Pursuing the Real

195 **"The point," he explains**: Norman Fischer, *Sailing Home* (Free Press, 2008), 79.

196 **Do not get carried away:** Eihei Dogen, *Tenzo Kyokun* (*Instructions for the Cook*), quoted in Kosho Uchiyama Roshi, *How to Cook Your Life: From the Zen Kitchen to Enlightenment* (Shambhala, 2005), 47.

When we have developed this kind of attitude: *How to Cook Your Life*, 49.

Back to School

198 **Once in a while you should stop:** Shunryu Suzuki, *Not Always So* (HarperCollins, 2002), 51-52.

199 **Old knowledge is the obstacle:** Thich Nhat Hanh, *The Sun My Heart* (Parallax, 1988), 50-51.

The Leaves' Fossils

206 **If what we see could forget us:** Elizabeth Bishop, "Quai d' Orleans," *The Complete Poems: 1927-1979* (Farrar, Straus and Giroux, 1984), 28.

207 **Do not pursue the past:** Thich Nhat Hanh, *Our Appointment with Life: Discourse on Living Happily in the Present Moment* (Parallax, 1990), 6.

What Were You Thinking?

209 **A guide to wise and harmonious living:** Thich Nhat Hanh, *The Heart of the Buddha's Teaching* (Parallax, 1998), 55-58.

Hope Is Not a Plan

212 **Like many people:** Atul Gawande, "Letting Go," *The New Yorker,* July 26, 2010. (http://www.newyorker.com/reporting/2010/08/02/100802fa_fact_gawande).

214 **Sounds terrible, doesn't it:** Charlotte Joko Beck, *Everyday Zen* (HarperSanFrancisco, 1989), 66, 68.

Children from the Sun

216 **"She fell asleep in the sun":** Pearse Hutchinson, "She Fell Asleep in the Sun," *An Anthology of Modern Irish Poetry,* ed. Wes Davis (Harvard University Press, 2010), 183-4.

The Life I Have Been Given

222 **With gratitude I remember:** Jack Kornfield, *The Wise Heart* (Random House, 2008), 399-400.

223 **Whatever it is:** Saigyo, "Gratitude," tr. Sam Hamill, *Gratitude* (BOA Editions, 1998).

Habits of Mind

225 **Technique, like the body's memory:** Glenn Kurtz, *Practicing: A Musician's Return to Music* (Knopf, 2007), 76.

226 **Too exposed, naked:** Pema Chodron, *Taking the Leap: Freeing Ourselves from Old Habits and Fears* (Shambhala, 2009), 9.

Andres Segovia's rendition of "El Noi de la Mare" may be heard on YouTube at *http://www.youtube.com/watch?v=Pb1 MNUoJg6c&feature=related.*

Leaning into the Curves

228 **A natural the way she rode:** Richard Russo, *Bridge of Sighs* (Knopf, 2007), 475.

229 **Step Two. Pause:** Pema Chodron, *Taking the Leap: Freeing Ourselves from Old Habits and Fears* (Shambhala, 2009), 40.

230 **One of the elements of research:** "The Healing Power of Mindfulness," *Shambhala Sun* (January, 2011), 49.

Effortless Effort

233 **The root of delusion:** Menzan Zuiho Zenji, "Jijuyu-zanmai" ("Samadhi of the Self"), in *Shikantaza: An Introduction to Zazen*, edited and translated by Shohaku Okumura (Kyoto Soto-Zen Center, 1985), 106.

The AeroPress was invented by Alan Alder in 2005. For more information please see http://en.wikipedia.org/wiki/AeroPress.

ABOUT THE AUTHOR

Poet and essayist Ben Howard was born in 1944 and grew up in eastern Iowa. His interest in Buddhist meditation originated in the 1970s, kindled by the prose of Peter Matthiessen and the poems of Gary Snyder. Having learned the fundamentals of sitting practice from Allen Ginsberg in 1978, he became a student of Vipassana meditation and later of Vietnamese Rinzai Zen, as taught by the Venerable Thich Nhat Hanh. More recently, he has studied Japanese Rinzai Zen with Jiro Osho Fernando Afable and Shinge Roko Sherry Chayat Roshi. In 2002 he received the *jukai* precepts in the Hakuin/ Torei lineage of Rinzai Zen at Dai Bosatsu Zendo.

Before his retirement in 2006, Howard taught literature, writing, and classical guitar at Alfred University. His numerous books include *Leaf, Sunlight, Asphalt* (Salmon Poetry, 2009), the verse novella *Midcentury* (Salmon, 1997), and *The Pressed Melodeon: Essays on Modern Irish Writing* (Story Line Press, 1996). He lives with his wife, Robin Caster Howard, in the village of Alfred, New York.

CPSIA information can be obtained at www.ICGtesting.com
Printed in the USA
BVOW010507200312

285571BV00001B/36/P